Unsent Letters

Unsent Letters

writing as a way to resolve and renew

Lauren B. Smith

WALKING STICK PRESS
Cincinnati, Ohio
www.writersdigest.com

Visit our Web site at www.writersdigest.com for information on more resources for writers.

To receive a free weekly e-mail newsletter delivering tips and updates about writing and about Writer's Digest products, register directly at our Web site at http://newsletters.fwpublications.com.

06   05   04   03   02   5   4   3   2   1

Library of Congress Cataloging-in-Publication Data

Smith, Lauren
   Unsent letters: writing to resolve and renew / by Lauren Smith.
     p. cm.
   Includes index.
   ISBN 1-58297-078-5 (alk. paper)
    1. Self-disclosure—Problems, exercises, etc. 2. Letter writing—Psychological aspects. 3. Catharsis. I. Title.

  BF697.5.S427 S65   2002
  158.1—dc21
                                       2001046881
                                         CIP

Edited by Kim Agricola and Meg Leder
Designed by Sandy Conopoetis Kent
Cover by Joanna Detz
Cover photo by Paul Taylor/Getty Images
Production coordinated by Sara Dumford
Author photo by Virginia Mann

I dedicate this book to my parents
who taught me what it means to write a letter
and what it means to love.
And I extend deep and sincere thanks
to the men and women who allowed their
heartfelt, revealing letters to appear
on the pages of this book.

ABOUT *the* AUTHOR

 During the course of her writing career, Lauren B. Smith has authored *The Visionary Pinhole*, a book about the art and history of pinhole photography, and worked as a freelance writer. She has taught English and creative writing courses, and created and edited *Messages From the Heart*, a quarterly journal dedicated to the experience of letter writing. It was from this journal and from her lifelong practice of using letters as a means of connecting with others and with her private self, that *Unsent Letters* was born. Lauren lives in an authentic adobe home in Tucson, Arizona.

TABLE *of* CONTENTS

FOREWORD

Arthur A. Stone, Ph.D.
Professor and Vice Chair
Department of Psychiatry and Behavioral Sciences
State University of New York at Stony Brook

There are many ways of knowing the world. The contemporary gold standard for "knowing" is the scientific paradigm—that is, when the data are gathered, analyzed, and interpreted using methods and rules that are cumulatively referred to as the scientific method. For many questions facing society, especially ones relating to the expenditure of public monies, as in health-care programs or other public benefit programs, this may indeed be a reasonable and proper standard. But when it comes to making decisions about how to maximize personal well-being and happiness, how to live a moral life, how to be fulfilled at a deep level, science typically offers little guidance. Inner peace is achieved by means not validated by science; in fact, some even say that such concepts should not be subjected to the scientific approach. How often do we look toward science to confirm our choice of spouse, spiritual life, occupation, or, more mundanely, leisure-time activities? Not often and for good reason—science has made almost no progress exploring these topics.

Recently, however, scientific methods have been applied to topics that were formerly "off-limits," topics such as religion, bio-energy, faith, morals, and healing. Although the jury is still out—and probably will be for some time—there are emerging hints that peoples' opinions about these topics, their views and beliefs, influence health and well-being.

But for now, I imagine that I have been asked to write the foreword for this book because I am a scientist with an interest in how writing about emotionally important events affects health. I study topics that fall into a field called behavioral medicine, specifically, about how emotions are determined and how they influence our physiology and our health. Let me describe how I decided to become involved with the writing about traumatic events, then share my reaction to *Unsent Letters*.

In the 1980s I served on the editorial board of a well-respected scientific journal and was expected to provide critiques of papers submitted to the journal for possible publication. One day I received a letter from one of the journal's editors with a somewhat unusual request: Would I be willing to serve as a "swing" reviewer for a paper that had received one enthusiastic review and one very negative review?

"Sure," I replied, and with my curiosity peaked dove into the paper—after all, it is uncommon for a scientific report to evoke such disparate reactions. I was excited by the results of the paper and also understood why it had evoked the contradictory views found in the prior reviews. The issue was this: A very brief psychological task based on writing about past traumatic experiences was shown to be associated with large improvements in health. Now I understood the controversy—the writing task was apparently producing salutary health effects that were equal to or greater than those previously shown with established one-on-one psychotherapies. How could this be? And, if it was true, what did it mean for the established therapies? The threat was clear. For me, the editorial conundrum was also clear; either I disbelieved the results, essentially implying some sort of scientific mischief, or I accepted the exciting results, knowing that they would surely result in controversy. On the basis of my review, this article was published in the journal.

This was the difficult, yet ultimately happy, journey of one of Dr. Jamie Pennebaker's early studies on writing and the inception of my own interest in the phenomenon. Pennebaker, one of psychology's avant-garde thinkers, is a pioneer in the scientific study of writing. His many studies have shown that various physiological systems are activated by writing about past traumatic experiences, that only certain types of writing produce the effect, and that health appears to improve after people write. Other scientists, including my colleagues and me, have tested the effect of writing in patients with serious medical illnesses to provide evidence to the medical community that writing is worthy of including as an adjunct to standard treatments. One of these notable efforts is mentioned by Ms. Smith. In a 1999 study in the *Journal of the American Medical Association*, we demonstrated that writing produced lower rates of disease activity as rated by their physicians in people with rheumatoid arthritis and that it improved objectively assessed lung function in asthma patients. It is worth noting that in this and in similar writing studies, the proportion of people who report past trauma is very high, suggesting the importance of developing treatments to deal with the trauma's lingering effects. Furthermore, let me also mention that anecdotal reports from participants in our studies indicate that many people enthusiastically say that the writing task has been beneficial.

I suggested earlier that science sometimes lags behind our desire for action; after all, it takes time to explore new possibilities for improving our health and well-being with the scientific method. This will probably always be the case. Yes, there is scientific evidence that writing may be an effective way to improve our health, at least in the short-term, but we are far from a full understanding about how this works or what works most effectively.

Here is where *Unsent Letters* comes into the picture. *Unsent Letters* should be thought of as a user's guide for therapeutic writing. The volume provides step-by-step instructions for therapeutic writing wherein models are provided, pitfalls in the writing process are flagged, and hints for a successful and satisfying writing experience are suggested. I enjoyed the friendly prose and especially appreciated the quotes that the author has placed at the beginning of each chapter from literary and philosophic luminaries. As it turns out, these literary giants appeared to have already discovered the utility of journal writing for themselves. I thoroughly enjoyed these quotations, marveling at the wisdom of the ancients, and I imagine that you will, too. For those who regularly journal, the book provides numerous variations on themes that will enhance the writing experience and bolster you if you become bogged down. Ms. Smith supplies the reader with a complete road map for constructing unsent letters in an imaginative and creative manner. Her thoughtful and beautiful letters suggest solutions for grappling with life's important and difficult issues. Who hasn't ignored the small tuggings of our unconscious mind? Ms. Smith recommends that we bring the obvious and not so obvious aspects of daily life into clear resolution, focusing our thoughts and feelings with writing letters to ourselves.

I cannot say for certain what science will discover about structured writing, but I do have a good sense that writing in the ways suggested by Ms. Smith has a bright future. In addition to the potential health benefits that may be realized with writing, the writer is certain to achieve a deeper awareness of oneself and that, in my view, is reason enough for reading this book.

INTRODUCTION: LETTERS, MY LIFELINE

The birth of this book goes back to 1958, the year I entered boarding school several towns away from my home. Being separated from my family and neighborhood during the tender years of adolescence was anything but easy on my wildly zigzagging emotions. I felt like a fledgling not ready to be torn from the nest and, at the same time, like a young woman wishing to be free and self-sufficient. It was during this boarding school experience that letters became a lifeline for me between school and home. These years were a time of growing up and growing away, as I held on to home and family via the delicate, precious tether of the written word.

Although many other details about that period of time have faded, I can well remember walking back to the dorm after classes, anticipating a letter in my mailbox as the late afternoon sun slipped down toward the earth. Seeing an envelope nestled in the wooden cubicle caused my heart to beat a little faster and my stomach to flip-flop. I would carry the precious gift to my room, kick off my shoes, sit cross-legged on my bed, and slide into comforting visions of home. Oh, the smiles that came with the stick figures my father had drawn on the envelope. Limericks would be there, too. "There was an old man in a hearse, Who murmured, 'This might have been worse; Of course the expense, Is simply immense, but it doesn't come out of my purse.'" I was certain that the postmen and my housemother had both enjoyed Dad's humor before it landed in my hands.

Inside the envelope would be my mother's message. As I read her words, I could picture her at the cherry, drop-leaf table in our kitchen. I could hear robins singing in the crabapple tree just outside the window at her shoulder. I envisioned her head bent over the tablet as she described the breaded pork chops and mashed potatoes with gravy she was making for dinner. I relished in news about my older brother and his high school friends, and about my younger sister and the games she was playing on the front stoop with Patty and Mary Ann. Mom would tell me news of Mitzi, our neighbor who played Frankie Yankovic records so loudly every Sunday morning we could have polkaed to her music in our kitchen had we wanted to. She'd tell me about Frank and Pauline's new car and about Edna and Eleanor inviting us up the hill to their house for Sunday dinner. There'd be news about Gramma and Grampa Widmer, Aunt Mudge and Uncle Johnny, and our other relatives who lived a long drive away on the West Side. And of heavy snowfalls and their early morning shoveling so that Dad could get to the factory on time. Letters would promise Dad's crispy potato pancakes during my next visit home. The glorious details of Mom's letters filled the empty space in my heart that echoed with the distance between school and home.

From those years on, letters have been as much a part of my life as wearing turtlenecks in the wintertime. It's something I do because it feels comfortable and oh, so right. I write letters. I receive and save letters. Early on I began to write to myself in my diary, carefully chosen for its miniature lock and key. I learned early in my life that writing was a way of not just connecting with other people, but a way of connecting with parts of myself that I could not reach through any other activity. Writing to myself in my diary was a way of lessening the sadness of being far from home. It was a way of sorting through confusing emotional swings that left me feeling disconnected from myself or others. When I was able to put words to my feelings, the power that the emotions held over me diminished. Before I wrote about a problem, my feelings had the upper hand. They were in charge, and there was nothing to do but rise and fall on their tides. But when I carried on a written dialogue with myself, I looked my disappointment, confusion, hurt, resentment, anger, and loneliness in the eye and talked to these feelings as if they and I could come to more comfortable terms. Writing about my feelings was a way of letting go of them, a way of redefining the power they held over me.

Messages Straight From the Heart

Letter writing and journaling continued to be so magical and meaningful a part of my life that in 1993 I created *Messages From the Heart*, a quarterly journal dedicated to these genres. The heartfelt writings from around the world that found their way onto this publication's pages during its seven-year life led directly to the book you are now reading. During the life of *Messages From the Heart*, new medical research was published that supported the long-held belief that writing can be a cathartic activity. For the first time, scientific investigation gave evidence that writing enables a person to process a traumatic event, to confront beliefs and give new meaning to them, and to gain a new sense of control and improved sense of self. Writing, in essence, gives us the chance to rewrite the belief system that shapes, and sometimes weighs down, our lives.

The backbone of *Unsent Letters* is a belief that we are capable of change and that, by writing private letters not meant to be sent, we are able to look our beliefs in the eye and ask whether the reality that informs our lives is working for us. If it is not, we can conduct a private dialogue with our individual beliefs, challenging them and discovering how they might be holding us back, causing us pain, and clouding our dreams. We can rename and reform our beliefs, wiping away old definitions or ineffective demands upon ourselves that no longer suit. And we can uncover a sense of our stronger, truer selves as we work through the process of writing toward becoming healthier, happier individuals. Natalie Goldberg puts this concept beautifully in her book *Writing Down the Bones* when she says, "The ability to put something down—to tell how you feel about an old husband, an old shoe, or the memory of a cheese sandwich on a gray morning in Miami—that moment you can finally align how you feel inside with the words you write; at that moment you are free because you are not fighting those things inside. You have accepted them, become one with them."

Writing letters that are not meant to be sent is a lesson in creativity. The practice is like walking round and round emotions, experiences, attitudes, and beliefs in order to see each from many points of view. Creativity stems from an inquisitive mind. And the inquisitive mind does not rest with nagging fear, anxiety, anger, loneliness, or regret. It wants to see the emotion as it relates to everything around it. It wants to pull the emotion from where it grows to examine its roots. The creative mind does not accept the emotion as it appears in early morning light but wants to see it under the hot noontime sun, and then illuminated by a full moon at midnight.

Aiming Toward Resolution

The exercises included in this book work toward creative unraveling. They work toward breaking down complex, overwhelming emotions into smaller, more understandable fragments. The process is somewhat like studying an unsettling piece of art. You examine the artwork inch by inch for clues as to its meaning. You see how the details work together, how the colors convey mood, how the light in the image reveals or conceals, how the use of paint hides or reflects the artist's presence. You dissect and study the tiny details in the artwork and gradually arrive at the place where you can deal with and understand the whole.

In the same way, you will write letters as you make your way through the following chapters, dissecting and closely studying various aspects of your emotional self as a way of working through stuck places in your life that overwhelm and, sometimes, frighten you. At times you will write a series of letters back and forth to yourself, to someone you know, or to an event or feeling. Sometimes you will write and rewrite one particular letter, watching the changes that take place in the rewrites, and making note of the awakening that is happening as you polish and rework your thinking and feelings about the subject of your letters.

In the final chapter of this book, you will be encouraged to take an important additional step—to write and send a letter that you have been avoiding. At this point you will have gained insight and let go of emotional baggage. Now, you will be ready for this final exercise. You will understand the source of the attitudes and emotions that have chiseled the shape of your days. You will have examined your beliefs and feelings in such a way that they no longer control your every action and thought. You will be ready to communicate with one or more people in your life about what you have learned. This concluding letter (or letters) might grow naturally out of the writing you have done for one of the chapters in this book. You may write to the friend with whom you had an argument, to your spouse with whom communication has become difficult, to a parent who long ago hurt you, or to a child with whom you have grave misunderstandings.

The letters you will write and send as a result of this last chapter will be a natural progression of the growth that has taken place through your writing exercises. For after you have opened your heart to yourself and have seen that everything you need exists there inside of you, you are ready and able to open your heart and share your beliefs with those closest to you. None of this is any easier than riding a bicycle for the first time or climbing beyond the rise in front of you to a faraway summit that feels out of reach. But every great accomplishment begins with one step and with a measure of determination and commitment. So commit now to make your way through the following chapters. Whether you are a longtime writer of letters and journal entries or you are new to the art, you will find these exercises an exciting means of discovery and letting go.

Helpful Nudges Along Your Way

Unsent Letters is designed so that you can either work from chapter one to the end of the book or tackle chapters as they relate to what is happening in your life. In chapter one, however, you will find helpful hints for getting started. Each chapter contains exercises with nudges to take you deeper and deeper into your feelings. The sample letters in each chapter are offered merely as inspiration, not as writing that you are meant to copy in form or content. You will notice that some of the sample letters are addressed to a person and were, in some cases, delivered. They have been included because they exhibit the sense of resolution that may come as you work through the exercises in this book.

Now it's time to begin. Read through the tips below, then turn to chapter one, pick up your pen, and write your heart out.

Tips to Assist Your Journey Through This Book

"And what, you ask, does writing teach us? First and foremost, it reminds us that we are alive and that it is a gift and a privilege, not a right. We must earn life once it has been awarded us. Life asks for rewards back because it has favored us with animation."
—Ray Bradbury, *Zen in the Art of Writing*

Write, write, and write some more

Return to the exercises in this book as many times as you wish. Remember that the ultimate goal in writing your "unsent" letters is to achieve resolution. Write, write, and write some more until your spirit exclaims, "Aha!" Write letter after letter, or write and rewrite one letter over and again until, all of a sudden, you possess insight that was hidden to you earlier. Write until you sense that you have achieved more peaceful, manageable attitudes about yourself, your beliefs, your feelings, your disappointments, your relationships, your place in the world. Write until you can put down your pen about that subject for a while and walk away with a lilt in your step. Then, sometime later, return if the spirit moves you to work further. The process is not one of a week or month. It is one of a lifetime.

Write in 3-D and Technicolor

Beginning with your very first "unsent" letter, be as specific as possible with your descriptions. In your first letter, you will address your favorite writing environment. Compare the colors, sounds, textures, and objects in this special place with something that is clearly under-stood. If the colors that awaken your inner voices are yellow and green, are they colors that remind you of buttercups and putting greens or of Poupon mustard and olives from Tuscany? Is the music that inspires you Vivaldi, Prince, or Tanya Tucker? If nothing like silence brings out the best in you, is this "sound" similar to that which you discovered at the bottom of the Grand Canyon or on a lake, fishing before dawn? Is it snuggling under your grandma's hand-crocheted afghan or sinking into an old leather chair that makes you feel at home enough to write your heart out? Beginning with the first letter you write in response to this book's exercises, describe the things you feel, remember, dream about, experience, and believe in. Use words, examples, and comparisons that take you to the core of what you mean to say and would take a reader clear to the center of your heart.

Choose a journal that reflects your mood

Choose your journal deliberately. A fancy, expensive blank book might stop you before you begin. Too fine a format may make you feel as though what you write must be monumental or perfect. On the other hand, elegance may inspire you with its seriousness. Whether you choose something exquisite or inexpensive, make certain that the pages lie flat for ease of writing. A 5″ × 7″ artist sketch-book with a spiral binding makes an inexpensive, easy-to-write-in, easy-to-take-with-you journal. Both plain and fancy blank books are available at bookstores, stationery shops, and art supply stores.

Safeguard your privacy

The privacy of letters is sacred. Remember this as you work through the exercises in this book. The only way you can be totally honest with yourself is to know without a doubt that only you will read what you write. Write in your private place, not under the nose of someone who will want to read your words. Hide your journal if you must. Create a time, place, and circumstance that provide you with total privacy. Then, let your words flow.

Be on the watch for internal clues

Entitle a page in your journal "Emotional Aha's," and make note of involuntary clues as they appear now and then as you work through the exercises in this book. When, from out of the blue, you cry, smile, laugh, feel raw in the pit of your stomach, or shiver with new insight, jot down when, where, how, and why you responded as you did. Define the situation, the words, sights, sound, touch, or aroma that caused the response. Be on the lookout for these unexpected emotional reactions because they provide useful glimpses of feelings that hide from view. They provide information about how you feel concerning relationships, yourself, and the world.

File your letters away as documentation of your growth

As always, date and save the letters you write. They will serve as evidence of emotional growth and development as you progress through this book.

Periodically, take a moment to give thanks for the work you are doing

Just as we take time to exercise and eat properly, to keep our house in order and our car running smoothly, we need to attend to our emotional well-being. After we do so, we gain great satisfaction in looking back over the time and energy we have spent tending to our spiritual selves. Take time now and then to write a thank-you to yourself about the inner peace and strength that you are building as you work through the exercises in this book. Remind yourself that you have come a long distance on your journey, and promise to continue this work that is making a difference in the quality of your life.

CHAPTER ONE

Setting the Stage and Getting Started

"In every encounter with reality the structures of self and world are interdependently present. The most fundamental expression of this fact is the language which gives man the power to abstract from the concretely given and, after having abstracted from it, to return to it, to interpret and transform it. The most vital being is the being which has the word and is by the word liberated from bondage to the given."
—Paul Tillich, *The Courage to Be*

The journal is well established as being an effective vehicle for working out the emotional kinks in your life. However, sometimes the blank journal page stares back at you defiantly. The more you need to write about how you feel, the harder it is to find words that would explain. While your thoughts repeat over and over in your head like a broken record about a bothersome issue, you find it impossible to give solid, written definition to the problem. But now, with this book, you are offered suggestions that will carry you over the speed bumps that separate you from the place where your heart speaks.

Instead of facing a blank page and wondering how to begin, you will write letters, addressing whatever it is that causes you concern as if you and that concern were old friends sitting together over a cup of coffee. Your deepest concern of the moment may be a person whom you need to forgive or from whom you need forgiveness. The thing that troubles you and needs your attention may be a parent or friend who has caused you hurt. It may be a disease that has changed your life or an opportunity that you hoped for but that did not materialize. A lost job, an ailing spouse, a natural disaster, an unfortunate accident, a lack of confidence—such life experiences cause hurt and confusion that need attention.

By writing letters that are meant to remain private, you are able to speak with total honesty and frankness about your feelings. No holding back. No censoring. No rewriting. No pausing. No worrying about spelling, grammar, or cleverness. You merely let the emotions flow toward the person, object, or event which sits like a rock in your heart. You talk to your fear or to your friend who has left you. You address your anger or your grief. Through writing letters, you sit eye to eye with your illness or with your spouse with whom you have lost closeness. You carry on a dialogue that eventually pulls you out of the rut in which you have been stuck for too long.

Your journal is as private as your heartbeat. Just as you symbolically think of your heart as the wellspring of your love and emotions, think of your journal as your secret vessel that you can fill with thoughts and feelings you share with no one else. Think of your journal as your center, as your retreat to which you can escape when you need peace or release from old hurts and resentments, when you want to build dreams or regain confidence. Think of your journal as the place where you are able to give voice to your most private self in order to sift through confusion, rid yourself of pain, confess the breadth of your love, plan for the future, or ask for forgiveness from yourself and others.

Your private, back-and-forth, written conversation with a person, feeling, situation, or event will enable you to sort through your emotions and understand them as you never have before. As you continue to write your unsent letters, the feelings that have weighed you down for too long will begin to shrink. Sending the emotions to your private page will give you a sense of control over them and over your life. You are in the driver's seat with the problem now. You are wrapping your own solid words around your concern rather than letting it gallop unfettered through your mind and heart. As you package the problem in a definition that fits, the power it held over you will diminish just as the power of a dream lessens as you awaken to a new day. You will feel physically larger than the problem for the first time in many moons.

At the same time, by refraining from sending a message of anger, hurt, resentment, or frustration to the recipient, you focus on your own growth and development rather than passing the negative energy along. You examine the problem and your reactions to it from all sides by writing private, unsent letters. Then, one day, you awaken feeling wiser, stronger, and ready to move on. You have let go of old, out-of-date issues. You have rewritten your personal story in terms that benefit your well-being, and move forward a healthier, stronger you.

Define the Nest From Which Your Spirit Soars

"Something soft and wild and free, something that whispered to the ear on the pillow, lightened the heart, softly, softly picked the lock, slid the bolts, and released the prisoned spirit of man into the wind, into the blue and gold, into the morning, into the morning."
—Willa Cather, *Death Comes for the Archbishop*

The writing that you will be doing is all about attaching new words and feelings to beliefs, people, places, and events. It is about *you* realizing your internal strengths, preferences, dreams, and choices. It is about taking one small step, then another, and another along the road marked "Letting Go."

As your first step on this road, you will define the writing environment that promotes your honesty and openness. The space should feel private and safe to you. It should be the sort of place that makes you feel alive and totally yourself. The place should feel as good to you as a warm den feels to a grizzly bear, as a nest of twigs and feathers feels to a mother robin, and as a wide-open sea feels to a walrus.

Picture an environment that helps you feel free and easy with your thoughts and open with your feelings. What details about this space make you feel at home and inspired? Does lighting a candle or placing a fragrant plant on your writing table inspire you to spread your wings? Does pouring yourself a cup of herbal tea or of steaming Kona coffee make you feel as though something good is about to happen? Does filling the air with soothing classical music or rocking rap make you feel as though your muse is hovering within reach? Since much of reality lies beyond the conscious level, you may not realize why you are drawn to a certain environment and repelled by another. Doing an exercise like this one will offer a deeper, broader view of who you are and what type of environment you wish to create around you.

Exercise 1: Speak Quietly to Your Private Space

Contemplate the power of your writing place by composing a letter to it in your journal. As demonstrated in the sample letter that follows, the dialogue that you begin between yourself and your room will take its own course if you let it flow. Begin your letter by defining what it is that comforts and inspires you to be open with your thoughts and feelings. Choose one object, one color, one texture or aroma. It may be the sunlight that flows into your room, the view from your window, or the symbolic window itself that holds meaning for you. It could be the worn carpet under your feet whose magic carries you to a land beyond the clouds. Perhaps the chair you sit in or the desk at which you write connects you with the spirit of those who sat and wrote there before you. You may wish to emphasize the special nature of this room by comparing it to an environment that blocks your openness or that makes you feel uncomfortable.

Thank your special room for the positive energy it gives you. Promise that you will note, appreciate, and document the subtle changes that take place in your secret chamber when you return to it again and again, just as you will carefully note, appreciate, and document the changes that take place inside of you.

Continue to dialogue with your writing environment, addressing different objects in it, writing to it during different times of the day or night, until you feel as though you have thoroughly defined what it is in the environment that inspires you as does no other place on earth.

SAMPLE LETTER: FROM MY FILES.

My dear private study, I come to you for peace and release. Being here alone, with the telephone unhooked, the warm afternoon sun falling on my back, bees buzzing hungrily outside my window, and hundreds of my favorite books lining the shelves around me, I feel more at home than in any other place on earth. I look at some of the oldest books on the shelves and am transported back, over the years, to Upson Elementary School. I loved the aroma of that place. I loved the way its blackish brown, wooden floor squeaked under my white summer sandals as I made my way toward the children's section where I would search for a *Flicka, Ricka, and Dicka* adventure I had not yet read. I loved the hushed, reverent atmosphere of these rooms. And how wonderfully proud and part of the system I felt as I carefully signed my name on the check-out cards in the books I was about to take home with me. With my signature, I joined a special circle of readers. There was nothing so full of promise as a stack of library books held in my arms.

Oh, study, you remind me how much I have always loved books. You remind me of our living room in Euclid, Ohio, where my father brought books like *Treasure Island* to life for my sister, brother, and me. I can see him lovingly fingering the corner of the page as he read to us. *Treasure Island* is here in the room with me today. So are *Little Women, Gulliver's Travels, Blackbeard,* and so many other favorites. Mysteries from childhood, collections of poetry from high school, Shakespearean plays from college. Psychology books from early marriage, *Aperture* from my study of photography. My history is here, in these books. In the photographic portraits that line the walls. In the files that fill the drawers and the information stored on the computer. If someone wanted to know me through and through, they would learn more by examining this room than by searching through any other room in the house. Someone once asked me why I do not get rid of books once I read them. "Do you ever go back to read them again?" he asked. "Not often," I responded, "but I like having the books around me."

I save the letters I receive, too, and they poke their noses out of baskets and boxes on the shelves in front of me and hide in file drawers at my side. I wonder whether I like the books near me as proof that I've read them. Do I like the letters here to prove that I have dear friends and family that love me? Do I need the proof of the portraits on the wall to show that once I was a serious photographer? Or, this computer to prove that I write? What if this proof were not here? Am I most comfortable in this room because my traces are here? Even as I write this, I realize that my place of reverie is at a lake, far away in upstate New York. I float on a raft in this vision. No books are near. No people. No traces of what I have been, done, or accomplished. The place of my reverie is escape. It is a place of pure being. You, office, are not escape. You are question. You are pressure to keep producing, to do something, to fill this moment, to see, appreciate, capture, and create. You remind me that I might have done something in the past moment or past year, but that is not enough. You remind me of all that I have not done and all I have not learned, yet want to. You are both a comfort to me and a gentle nudge. It is not enough to have been, for there is today and so much more to experience and realize. I never thought of this before, but you are as much a symbol of my current moment waiting to blossom as you are a record of yesterday. And, because of what you are, you will not allow today to go empty. You visualize my restlessness. So, how can I say that you are my release or my peace? Perhaps only in feeling the passage of time—the history, the cycles that are evidenced in this room—can I feel peace, for through those cycles I experience change, growth, and meaning. Not in escape. Not in reverie. And so, my study, you offer me a sense of promise and of something far bigger than myself or my imagination, just as did the books my tiny arms carried home so many years ago.

Take the First Step Toward Turning Your Heart Inside Out

"Whatever the issue is that seems to block us from a full and satisfying life, identifying and verbalizing that obstacle is essential. For as long as it remains unconscious, it has far more control over us. . . . As long as the issue keeps arising, it serves us to acknowledge it, embrace it as who we are at present, and then let it go. Ironically, it seems, the more we acknowledge and embrace who we are—'warts and all'—the more likely we are to grow and eventually move beyond those blocks that impede us."
—Clare Cooper Marcus, *House as a Mirror of Self*

Exercise 2: Sketch Your Emotional Baggage

Now that you have described the environment that nurtures your openness and encourages you to write without censure or judgment, it is time to turn inward. During this exercise you will take a look inside at emotions you have buried out of habit. You will open yourself to experience both sorrow and joy to a greater degree. This will not be an easy exercise, for we are taught to stifle what is not pleasant, to avoid admitting weakness or pain. Since we were six we've been told to bike without training wheels, to pull ourselves up by our bootstraps, to keep a stiff upper lip, to show the world our strong side, to always be our best selves. It is not our habit to face the things inside that hurt or that feel quivery or small.

It is a known fact, however, that if we suppress negative emotions we also diminish our capacity to experience great joy. It is not possible to put a lid on some of our feelings without tamping down the rest of them. If, on the other hand, we confront emotions we would rather not face, we expand our ability to feel happiness. If there are emotions, memories, or experiences that eat away at us, we are much more likely to get the upper hand with them if we face them than if we turn our back on them.

Imagine yourself at age five trying to fall asleep with the bogeyman lurking nearby. You turn your back on the darkest part of the room. You think about your dog, the new book you brought home from the library, the ice-cream cone you had for dessert. But there is no enjoyment in thoughts of these sweet details of life, no rescue of sleep until your parent turns on the light and encourages you to look into all of the corners, under the bed, behind the chair, and inside the closet to see that there is, indeed, no hiding monster. It exists only in your thoughts.

Emotions are real when we feel them. At age five, fearing bogeymen or monsters in the night is legitimate and understandable. But turning away from any emotion works against us. The emotion hangs on and becomes a burden. Admitting to the bothersome emotion and going in search of its source gives us hope of putting feelings such as anger, fear, sadness, and regret in their rightful place as something we can control rather than something that controls us. Looking squarely at our emotions helps us feel more fully alive. Putting new words to experiences and memories helps us feel healthier and more in control.

In the nudges that follow, you will gain a broader, deeper view of who you are and how you would like your life to change for the better. A useful visual to employ while preparing to write these letters is to imagine that you are wearing a backpack. You have been carrying this heavy burden for such a long time that it seems part of you. You are accustomed to its feel and weight. You barely realize that the backpack is still there, and you certainly cannot remember its contents.

The backpack symbolizes the memory bank of hurt, pain, sadness, regret, anger, and other such negative emotions that we tend to shove down, down, down inside, as if by doing so we are able to move beyond them. But emotions do not wither with neglect, as Marcus suggests. Instead, they grow heavier in our backpack (or solar plexis). And, one day, we realize that we cannot take the weight any longer. The hindrance of the stored emotion pulls us to a halt, or it causes us to act in ways that surprise and dismay us.

Now imagine that you are climbing a mountain and lack the strength to go farther with the weight you are carrying in your pack. You must toss aside one item at a time to be able to proceed up the steep path. But first you must examine the contents of your emotional backpack to see which negative feelings you might discard. You lift one memory or feeling at a time to the light and examine it carefully. You decide what it has meant to you all these years and why you have continued to carry it with you for so long. Address the memory and the feelings attached to it directly as you would a person you knew long ago; this imprint has been with you just as an old friend's influence has remained a part of you even though you've been out of touch for a long time.

As you give names to the emotional baggage you have been

carrying, as you address the weighty memories or attitudes that keep you from being your best, something akin to magic will take place. The power of the emotions will diminish. Instead of their holding quiet, unseen power over you, you will take charge of them. As U.S. illustrator and metaphysicist Florence Scovel Shinn says, "We cannot always control our thoughts, but we can control our words, and repetition impresses the subconscious, and we are then master of the situation."

Nudge 1

Imagine yourself removing emotions from your backpack. Make a list of the hurts, resentments, regrets, feelings of sadness, fear, anger, and, yes, the feelings of strength and self-assurance that you carry with you as your self-definition. You may feel strong on the outside and enjoy showing the world the best and brightest *you*. But what is below the surface that is nagging at you? If you have trouble digging deep into your backpack, ask yourself questions like these: What was your last thought before falling asleep last night? What did your dreams tell you? How did you feel upon awakening this morning? What feelings surface when you go to work, shop for groceries, see your friend at lunch, call your child's teacher at school, talk to your husband or wife about this month's bills, telephone your parents to check on their health, read the mail that shows up in the postbox, work out at the gym or avoid exercise, prepare dinner? Picture yourself moving through yesterday and list the emotions you felt as you attended to your chores, jobs, and recreation. Go further back in time and picture yourself at a recent family gathering, at a business meeting or social event, and list the emotions that surfaced.

Nudge 2

Making a list is like sketching a drawing before beginning your watercolor. Help yourself dig deeper into the backpack by listing the five greatest stresses and five greatest comforts in your life and the emotions tied to them. List the five worst and five best experiences of your life and their corresponding emotions. List five things that make you happiest, saddest, weakest, strongest, most frustrated, gleeful, angry or inspired, frustrated or free. List your five happiest memories from childhood and your five most painful.

Because we are so caught up in our daily lives and in the things we need to accomplish to feel our best at the moment, it may be difficult to reach the feelings that have hidden below the surface for many months or years. The lists I suggest will help chip away at your defenses. They will help you examine the emotional backpack that is connected to the ache in your shoulders, the tightness in your jaw, or to the headaches or raw stomach that plague you periodically.

Nudge 3

It's time to write a letter to yourself. Begin it, "Dear [your name]." You may continue, "There is so much I want to say about how I am feeling today. So much that I have held inside and not expressed, even to myself." Or, begin your letter in your own words, writing from your heart about those emotions that appeared in your lists.

Write as if you are sitting across the table from yourself. Put a photograph of yourself on the table next to your journal so you can look into the eyes in the image and direct your comments there. Describe yourself in terms of the feelings you listed above. For your first letter, it may be a good idea to choose one of the emotions in the list and focus on it. Examine this one feeling from all angles. Does this emotion emerge only when you are with certain people or only in specific places or situations? When you feel this emotion welling up inside of you, does your reaction to it remind you of someone else—perhaps your father, mother, brother, or child? Do you feel as though you inherited your reaction to the emotion from someone? If so, who? Has your reaction to this feeling changed over the years? Do you hide this emotion? Do your dreams reflect this emotion? Do you go to see movies or read books that make this emotion come alive in you? What do you like and hate about this emotion?

Write as though the image of yourself in the photograph is someone you have not seen in a long time. Tell this person about the concerns that fill your heart and mind. Know that this person wants to hear every detail and will listen with an understanding heart. Write and write and write. Do not hold back. Let the words flow from your heart to the paper. Talk about the things in your life that keep you awake at night, that make your stomach ache and bring tears to your eyes. Talk about those things that cause you to feel (or act) three years old again, that cause you to steam or scream, that stress or comfort you. Try to present your total emotional self. Doing so may take more than one letter, but keep writing until you feel as though you have offered a complete sketch of the internal you.

SAMPLE LETTER: FROM KIM SANWALD-REIMANIS, KALAMAZOO, MICHIGAN. KIM SAYS, "LETTERS TO MYSELF, WRITTEN DURING A SERIOUS BOUT OF DEPRESSION, ASSISTED ME ON MY SPIRITUAL JOURNEY."

Dear Kim,

I walked through the threshold of my sanctuary and noticed the paper whites I have planted starting to bloom. I marvel at the tiny white flower just opening, reaching for the light coming through the window. Two weeks ago this flower was a small, brown, unassuming bulb. This I nestled between stone and water, totally confident it would bloom, glancing at it now and then for confirmation of a vague faith in nature and its course. I stare at the small flower, touch its smooth stem, take in its musky scent and feel its presence on some deeper, unexplained level. Behind the paper whites there is frost on the window duplicating a forest of ferns I'm sure I saw last spring. I am struck by the silence of this gift and its patience with me. Its beauty not dependent on my noticing it. I feel an unexpected sense of grace, and my eyes fill with tears. I am caught off guard by my emotion. I am humbled by the mystery of life and know I am not meant to understand it all.

During walks, hiking, and solitude, I am able to intuit a strong nonverbal connection to the bigger picture. A sense of being held surrounds me, and for a brief moment I am at peace.

I am noticing how much I'm defined by my relationship with others. Wife, friend, co-worker, sister, each one complete with its own set of assumptions and definitions. I seem to be at times a different person to my husband, than to my brothers, than to my friends. This fragmentation does not allow me to get a clear picture of myself. I also see in terms of relationship, just how much power I give to how others define me. Their praise inflating and affirming, their criticism debilitating and wounding. I am all or nothing, totally dependent on outside input to which my psyche reacts accordingly. Without this mirroring of others, how do I know what I look like?

During times of depression I have been unable to explain the seductive quality of this inner space. Through the process of solitude and letter writing, I am discovering who I am in relation to myself, the light and darker qualities. My anger and despair no longer shut me outside myself. They are signals for me to dig deeper in my efforts to uncover my gold. I know it is there, shining, waiting to be found.

Yesterday when looking for something else, I discovered the first letter I wrote to my mother, six months before her death. I hadn't remembered keeping a copy of it. It is a letter containing my first step toward separation from her dominance, putting me at the threshold of my soul's labyrinth. Shimmering like heat on the road in front of me, my writing is ultimately about my relationship between myself and Spirit.

Relationship. My illusion of separateness comes into clarity, the endless years of self-imposed exile from life. I feel pregnant with ideas. The metaphor of birth runs too parallel to this whole process to be ignored. My life's choices being necessary for gestation to occur. Feeling misunderstood by others all my life, I misunderstand myself and the sacredness of my being.

My writing has allowed me to shift into a much larger, more confident and motivated space. As I walk toward myself, I learn the meaning of responsibility. I am learning to love with mere honesty. I cannot rest until I see my world clearly.

Love, Kim

Awaken to the Promise of Your New, Best Self

> *"Morning is when I am awake & there is a dawn in me. . . . We must learn to reawaken & keep ourselves awake, not by mechanical aids, but by an infinite expectation of the dawn, which does not forsake us in our soundest sleep. I know of no more encouraging fact than the unquestionable ability of man to elevate his life by conscious endeavor. It is something to be able to paint a particular picture, or to carve a statue, and so to make a few objects beautiful: but it is far more glorious to carve and paint the very atmosphere and medium through which we look . . . to affect the quality of the day, that is the highest of arts."*
> —Henry David Thoreau, *Walden*

Beginning the day like a sprinter breaking from the starting block feels right and good to some. But to others, greeting the morning is best done by honoring the soul. I know a man who, first thing every day, reads inspirational messages in a quiet place and then recites one of his own poems to fortify his spirit. I know of one woman who begins her mornings with herbal tea and journal writing. Some people take a quiet walk in a garden. Some meditate. Some lie in bed, saying a prayer of thanks as the sky comes to life. Some begin the day with meditation, some with a song. The most important thing about beginning the day is to realize what a gift it is to receive another twenty-four hours of life and to give thanks in our own way for this time.

Exercise 3: Write to the Dawn of Your Self-Discovery

The way you begin your day can be totally your design. It may require awakening a little earlier than usual to take command of the day's first moments. Beginning the day as you wish to, rather than feeling as though someone else is writing the morning script, enables you to feel as though you awaken on a powerful note. It fortifies you to design the rest of the day . . . and the rest of your life. This step of taking charge of your morning is symbolic of a first step in taking charge of your emotional life. As Paul Tillich says in *The Courage to Be*, "Man creates what he is. And the courage to be as oneself is the courage to make of oneself what one wants to be." So, make the first few moments of the day totally your own. Realize as you do that your entire life is yours, as well.

Taking this first step is not difficult. It just requires choice, heart, a little time, and refraining from contemplating the entire journey. Who knows where this particular journey will end? Besides, getting there is not the goal. The goal is to live fully along the way. So get out your journal and your pen, feel the promise that comes with a new day, and define how it is that you will greet each morning that is given to you.

Nudge 1

Write a letter to the day's beginning: "My dear sweet morning." Write to it as if you love it, even if you don't consider yourself a morning person. Write to the morning, thanking it for being there for you, the start of a new, uncharted, exciting twenty-four hours. Tell the morning that you truly deserve to begin the day in your very own way, not according to someone else's plan. Tell the morning that no matter what happens after your unique beginning of the day, you will be strengthened and renewed by your morning ritual. Then describe how you will begin each day from now on. Be as specific as possible. Describe why you love your rite of the dawn. Tell how your unique jump-start to the day makes you feel. Did you learn this celebration of the day from someone else or dream it up yourself? Ask the morning for the strength and wisdom you will need to stick to the morning ritual if someone criticizes, judges, or tries to sabotage your private time.

End your letter by thanking the morning for offering you this unique opportunity for active enrichment. With every step you take to deepen your understanding and to increase the feeling that you are in charge of your life, you strengthen your will to live in a happy, healthy fashion.

Nudge 2

Now that you have taken the first steps in this exciting journey of discovery, it's time to schedule regular sessions for unsent letter writing. You might wish to begin with twenty minutes three days a week. You might want to write for fifteen minutes each day. Perhaps one hour two days a week feels best to you. Whatever pattern you choose, enter it in ink on your calendar as you would your best friend's birthday party or lunch with relatives visiting from out of town. This commitment is the first important step in moving beyond your emotional roadblocks. By setting aside regular segments of time to write, you admit to yourself that you are capable of growth and that you are worthy of this special, private time for self-development. By setting aside regular time to write, you make a promise with yourself to work toward a healthier, happier you.

So, write a formal letter to yourself, stating where you are going to write, how often, and for how many minutes each session. Describe briefly why it is you are making this written contract with yourself and what results you expect from this commitment. Be specific and date your unsent letter so you can return to it later to remind yourself how, why, and where you began this journey and how far you've progressed toward your goals.

CHAPTER TWO

Reaching Out for Help

"We're all in this together . . . alone."
  —Lily Tomlin

S ome primitive peoples around the world believe they lose part
of their souls if someone makes a likeness of them with a
camera or in a drawing or painting. I didn't know about this belief
when I was a child, but I felt similar fears. I grew up thoroughly
convinced that if I told too much about myself, a part of me would
be lost in the process. I was certain that if I revealed more than
just a little about my innermost thoughts, I would be putting the
power that I needed to survive into someone else's hands. I would
lose my freedom. In essence, it would be like giving away a plastic
baggie of atoms that I had lifted from out of my heart. I grew up
believing that it was better to lock most of what I thought and
felt inside rather than laying my feelings bare before the world.

Until I was in my thirties, it felt good to be a private person.
Everyone that knew me accepted that I was quiet and reserved.
But then I hit the wall. Huge uncertainties developed in my head
and, instead of being able to sort quietly through my thoughts
and feelings on my own as I always had done before, I faced a
Gordian knot of emotions that defied unraveling. Not only did I
not know how to talk through my turmoil with another person,
but I believed that I should avoid this tactic at all costs. I turned
more and more inward and focused harder and harder on my

confusion. "I will solve this myself. I will solve this myself," I said silently like a mantra.

The more I tried to solve things on my own, the more desperate I felt. My habit of holding feelings inside was not working. I had to make a change, yet I didn't know how to open up. I remember feeling as though words filled my mouth like too much saliva while my lips held back the tide. I felt as though I were a vault whose key had never been made. My inner cries saw no way to freedom.

"One of the hardest things in life is having words in your heart that you can't utter."
—James Earl Jones

At this point I needed to break a lifelong pattern of behavior and realized that I couldn't do it on my own. I was fortunate to find a counselor through whom I learned to trust both my voice and the process of communication. He helped me shed the fear that something horrid would happen if I voiced my beliefs, fears, dreams, and uncertainties. Through him I experimented with verbalizing what I felt. Neither going to the counselor nor working through this huge stuck place in my life was easy. Many months passed before I went in search of help, and years passed during the process of learning how to communicate. Old habits are not broken easily. But the exploration unlocked a fear and taught me that seeking help was OK both in my everyday life and when problems arose that were too large to handle alone.

SAMPLE LETTER: FROM DANA ECELBERGER, MENDOCINO, CALIFORNIA. DANA CONTEMPLATES HER NEED FOR HELP.
To whom it may concern,

I'm thinking of yesterday; how I felt so permeable, penetrable. How the madness of the civilized world stood at my door in a self-righteous fit and demanded to be let in. My door seemed to be blown off its hinges, and I had no way of keeping anything out. The cars speeding bumper to bumper along the freeway, each with a solitary driver shuttered away—not unlike turtles hiding in their shells with a false sense of security. The shopping center that has been growing like a disease upon the belly of what used to be wetlands. The cellular phones, lines of fast-food restaurants, fast oil changes, fast checking, fast lanes. They all made me wonder if it were me who had gone crazy or everyone else. I wanted to park the truck in the parking lot of one of the many, many, obscenely many shopping malls, take a company check and write myself a few thousand dollars, and catch a plane to someplace far away where no one knows me, where no one has heard of America, and where they have a kind of reverence and cautiousness around the insane. I wanted to stop and call someone to drive down to get me, to feed me, to rock me back to sanity, but I didn't want to bother anyone I knew. I wanted to call my boss in that moment of hysteria and say, "Listen, I want you to understand I have hit the wall. I've come undone and I need a break now. Today. Please help me." I needed to give up. I needed to fall without breaking anything. I wanted to disappear behind my eyes, draw the shades and never again leave the house. I wanted to eat real food. But, there was no time for that. Instead I spoke in a very firm voice to the disintegrating woman and to the truthful eye, and I warned them and cajoled them and told them to just keep driving. And I cried because I'm so strong I cannot give up, even when continuing on is destroying me.

The notion of asking for help is foreign to many of us. We are taught to be self-sufficient; besides, it feels good to do things alone. "Look, Mom! I made this myself," says little Tommy with a beaming smile as he holds up a paper airplane and sends it soaring across the room. Great satisfaction comes with accomplishing, surviving, creating, solving, realizing, discovering totally on our own.

One of the most famous proponents of self-sufficiency was Ralph Waldo Emerson, who wrote extensively on the subject in the early 1800s. "Man is his own star," he said. "A man should learn to detect and watch that gleam of light which flashes across his mind from within, more than the luster of the firmament of bards and sages." In poetry and essays, Emerson extolled his fellow citizens to be independent, declaring, "Nothing is sacred but the integrity of your own mind."

We need to be independent to prove our uniqueness and to separate ourselves from our parents, siblings, friends, and mentors. When we do for ourselves, we demonstrate our talents, abilities, strength, determination, focus, and commitment. We show the world, and often ourselves, who and what we are and can be. Just last night a friend told me about a relative who recently had been diagnosed with a serious illness. The aunt insisted that life go on as usual. She did not want assistance and did not want discussion to circle around her condition. Her strongest instinct was to face her illness on her own and in her own terms as long as she could.

But needing help from others is just as human as wishing to handle life and its challenges independently. Sometimes the situation is too big to be tackled alone. Sometimes it is just too lonely to proceed without someone there working with you. The push and pull of wanting and not wanting help begins early. Picture a two-year-old who asks his mother to hold him one minute because he needs comfort and reassurance and, the next minute, pushes himself away so he can waddle across the room on his own pudgy, little legs. Picture the high school senior who begins to behave in strange and disagreeable ways because she is torn between escaping to college life and staying home where help and nurturing are close at hand.

Some people never learn to comfortably ask for help. They spend their lives proving that they are capable of a solo journey. Perhaps these folks trust themselves more than they do others. Asking for help demands trust, after all. We don't go to the dentist for help with a toothache without believing in this person's capabilities, nor to the doctor without feeling great trust in his or her expertise. Before we call a lawyer, a plumber, or a carpet cleaner, most of us ask friends for references. We need to believe in the expert we turn to before we are comfortable asking for help. But once we are ready, we find that asking for assistance becomes a gentle give-and-take. I would have experienced no help from my counselor without doing significant work myself. We do not heal by a doctor's hand alone but by taking good care of ourselves as well. When we turn to a lawyer to make out a will, he or she cannot complete the task without our valuable input. When you go to a photographer for a portrait, the expert pushes the shutter release but it's you who has to do the smiling.

Exercise 1: Consider the Positives of Asking for Help

"We cannot afford not to fight for growth and understanding, even when it is painful, as it is bound to be."
　—May Sarton, *Journal of a Solitude*

When we ask for help, we do not give away our power. We extend and magnify it by connecting our abilities with those of someone else. Asking for help is like joining hands with someone in whom we believe. Seeking help is recognizing the need for change and taking action to make it happen. It is a positive, not a negative, response to life, and it is one of the most human choices we can make.

Today you will write a letter asking for help. Even if you thoroughly believe that you need no assistance or support at this moment, complete the exercise so when you do need to turn to someone, you will have the tools to do so.

Nudge 1

Make a list of the many ways in which you already ask for help. For instance, you may turn to such people as a dentist, librarian, seamstress, baker, caterer, auto mechanic, hair stylist, gardener, bank teller, minister, repairperson, postal worker, grocer, photo processor, and teacher for assistance with things you cannot do yourself. List as many such people as come to mind. Describe in one sentence what each does for you. Then, choose several of these people, and make notes below each name as you consider the following questions:

- Was it difficult turning to any of these people for help? If so, why?
- Did you feel as though you trusted each to do a job correctly for you? Did you feel the same about the people after they'd finished their jobs?
- Were you tempted to do any of these tasks yourself? If so, why didn't you?
- Were you satisfied with the help or service each provided, and

did you return to any of them for additional assistance? If not, why?

- Could you have avoided turning to any of these people for help?
- What part in the process of receiving help did you play? Did a working relationship or friendship develop between you and any of these experts in the process? Do you feel as though you gave anything in return to any of these people other than monetary payment?

Nudge 2

Now write a letter to yourself describing your attitude toward asking for help. Consider these questions:

- In what situations has it been all right for you to reach out for assistance in the past?
- When has it not been all right? Why were you hesitant to ask for help in that situation?
- What was the last time you asked for help in a situation that felt major?
- In what situation did you not ask for help only to discover that you should have? What kept you from seeking help, and would you tackle the situation differently today?

In your letter, give yourself permission to ask for help when you need it. Your thoughts create the highest hurdle between you and the help you may need. Remind yourself that asking for help is a creative way to solve a problem. It means that you want to see a situation or challenge from as many viewpoints as possible. You want to break the challenge apart, examine its insides, explore its assemblage, and reassemble it in a way that makes more sense to you and that works better in your life. And working through this process with someone is more effective and meaningful and maybe even more comforting, interesting, or fun than working alone. Using such arguments, tell yourself that asking for help is not only a human action but also a smart one.

Exercise 2: Conjure an Image of Strength

Visualizing can be a stepping-stone to getting beyond a stuck place. A friend of mine once used the vision of a kind pair of eyes to be able to cross a footbridge over the Colorado River. Without that image to talk to and believe in, without that image beckoning her forward, she might never have made the journey. But focusing on something other than her fear of heights and of the cold water far below enabled her to cross the bridge and complete a hike through the Grand Canyon with her family.

Sometimes, when asking for help from a person is too difficult or when you are alone with your problem, you can call on a symbol of hope for its magic. This symbol can be the eyes of a kind person. It can be the mountains, a hummingbird, a religious icon, an ancestor, the man in the moon. It can be any object that symbolizes strength, wisdom, and hope for you.

Nudge 1
Use your instincts. Listen to your heart. Look around you to see what element of your environment provides a sense of calm and wonder. Choose a symbol that holds a sense of mystery and power for you. Then, write to your symbol of hope for twenty minutes, talking about your biggest concern in life at the moment. It may be a job, a relationship, an illness, a goal that seems unattainable,

a financial dilemma, a fear of flying that threatens to keep you from attending your sister's wedding. Whatever your concern of the day, talk to this symbol as if it were a wise, loving, and understanding counselor. Describe your greatest fear connected to this concern. Discuss the worst that could happen with this situation. Consider the advantages and disadvantages of asking for help with the problem. As you write, imagine that a connection is forming between you and your symbol and that your symbol is lessening the weight of your problem.

SAMPLE LETTER: FROM KATHERINE E. RABENAU,
MESA, ARIZONA.

Dear God,

Sometimes I am so tired of my journey, so tired of the terror that seems to own me, so tired of looking for the face of the enemy and seeing only darkness. I am so tired of shaking and shaking and gasping for breath, of feeling like something is out there waiting to kill me, but not knowing who or what it is. I am so tired, God, of having my body go rigid and my mind go numb. And I'm so very tired of being so alone with it, of wanting people to understand and knowing that they can't because even I don't understand.

I am ashamed. And at the same time I'm proud of this secret courage—to have lived and loved and strived with this horror ticking inside me. But now it seems to have the upper hand, and I live exiled behind a force field of power that no one else can see or feel. I'm so ashamed that I can't draw its face and cry, "See! See! There it is! Do you feel it? Now do you understand?" I am so tired of this war, of this lonely existence fighting shadows which are so real—despite their lack of substance—that they leave me worn and drawn and lost.

I want to give it all to you, God. I hereby do so, except I don't quite know how. But I give you my desire to give it to you. I give you my desire to be free to live and laugh and let my soul come out to play. I ask your help, God, because I don't seem to be getting very far on my own—or even with your help, which I keep asking for and which I think I'm getting. But even so, God, I'm so damned tired. And even with all the help I get, I still feel so alone. So I give you also my tiredness and my loneliness and my hope. I give you the dreams that are all locked up inside the cage of my fear. I want my dreams, God. I want to feel a sense of purpose. I want to be alive. I want to slay my fear, to let my rage fly out and strike the source and not be held inside anymore, eating at me. I want to be able to feel it and let it be OK.

Those bastards raped a baby, God, a little girl who didn't understand. They did such things to me and still I feel more bewildered than angry. Somehow, I still seem to think it was my fault, I guess. I don't know. I don't know why I can't get outside of it and put its ugliness to rest, put my pain to rest. I ask your help, God, because I'm tired. I've been working so hard and still they won't give me up. Or maybe I won't give them up. I don't know. So I give them up to you, God, right here, right now.

Please take them. Please take whatever or whomever inside of me that holds on to thinking that if I let go, I won't exist anymore. Maybe because if I keep holding on I can still pretend that it's not true, that it didn't happen. I can pretend that my parents took care of me, that they loved me so much they'd have felt my pain. I can pretend I felt wanted and safe and that this is just an aberration, a nightmare from which I'll soon wake up.

I give you my confusion, too, God. I give you my illusions about my mother. I give you the needs I learned not to have, the feelings I put to death. I give you my loneliness. I give you my needs and wants and desires, and I ask you to give them back to me, to let me have them and live and breathe and feel them. I give you my denial, and I ask you to help me face the truth. There's probably more, but that's enough for now. I give you my heart, too. I think it's broken. Can you please fix it?

Thank you, God, for listening, if for nothing else. With hope and despair,

Katherine

Nudge 2

Now, think of the same concern or another one that perplexes you as an intricately carved box that you can pick up, turn over, and examine. See yourself opening the box and looking inside where many tiny compartments hold secrets written on delicate paper. Imagine yourself unfolding the notes and reading the secrets. Write for twenty minutes about the secrets hidden in this box. As you do, continue writing to your symbol of hope. Write about the events, people, and places in the past that are linked to your current dilemma.

You may want to sketch the box as you examine it mentally, diagramming the compartments, coloring the layers and design of its exterior, labeling the secrets you discover inside. Describe what you discover about the nature of your problem and the role it plays in your life.

At the end of your writing session, ask your symbol for help, strength, and clarity with your dilemma. Return in writing to your symbol of hope for several days to discuss your problem and to practice using this mental image to gain a sense of comfort and strength. With repeated writing sessions, you will improve your ability both to visualize your symbol and to ask for help whenever you feel the need.

SAMPLE LETTER: FROM EILEEN BELL,
EL SEGUNDO, CALIFORNIA.

Dear Sparrow,

I began watching you years ago, when my father was dying. I don't know how it began, perhaps staring out through the kitchen window or on a walk at the botanical gardens or maybe sitting at the water's edge watching the waves' glassy recession over the sands of the shore. But there was a precise moment that you were born in me— the idea of flight or migration, the possibility of renewal even in the face of deep, deep sorrow.

I have watched you and your cousins, studied your movements, learned to identify you by your feathered markings. In my garden, I have found you eating the fruits of my labor, the peanuts, the sunflower and cosmo seeds, the suet that I hang from the eaves in winter. You have come, yellow and blue, mottled shades of brown. Always, always flattering me with your presence.

On one particular afternoon, I searched for you as my father lay in the ER, pain in his liver, cancer eating away at him. I left his side to seek you out. Walking the hospital grounds, my binoculars at my neck like an amulet. There had been many times I had searched for you in parking lots, along highways, at the perimeters of abandoned buildings. But on this day I walked beneath the palms and banyon trees perplexed at how I could be looking for you, seeking out something so small and fleeting as you, so unattached to my person, and finding some sort of happiness in this, knowing at the same time that I was losing him.

Oh, but you survive! You come to my yard, having found your way from clear across this continent. Each year, knowing when to arrive, when to take leave, without questioning why, without demanding a reason. This is how I needed to let him go. I needed to be like you, to nest and brood and feed and be released. To take wing when the season changed. And so, with your help, I let him go. I pull myself from sadness, hobble to the window to be in the sunlight again and to encounter your form in the bath or foraging beneath the ferns.

I have watched for you in dense forests, from the ledges of mountain cliffs, from the banks of rivers, peering, always peering for a glimpse of you. And always I find you. Always I give thanks. For you, my feathered savior, gave me back hope, and laughter, and courage, and the will to move on.

A woman

Exercise 3: Consider the Cost of Seeking Help . . . or Not Doing So

For the next step in the process of learning how to ask for help, you will write an unsent letter to someone from whom you would like help. In preparation for doing this, read the following questions, then put your pen down for a day. Let the questions steep in the warmth of your heart. Let them brew there like an herbal tea bag. When you pick up your pen tomorrow for Nudge #1, answers will flow onto the page. Consider:

- What is the risk to you, to your sense of pride or sense of self, if you ask for help? What is the risk if you do not?
- What sacrifice is connected to asking for help?
- What outcomes might you expect if you asked for help or refrained from doing so?
- What expectations will you take with you if you ask for help? Are your expectations clear in your mind? Are they realistic?
- How will you handle your emotions if you do not get the help you seek or the outcomes you expect? What will be your Plan B?
- How much time and energy are you willing to expend on the issue once you ask for help? Are you willing to work as hard or harder than the person from whom you ask for assistance?

Nudge 1

Spend twenty minutes writing to the person from whom you want help. Carefully explain the problem that faces you and your feelings about asking for help. Be precise, clear, and detailed in defining how your problem affects your life. Explain the help that you need, being specific about what you would like the person to do for you. Tell what it will mean to you to receive help. Discuss your answers to the questions at the beginning of this exercise. Outline your expectations so both you and the person to whom you are writing will know (1) what you want to happen once you receive the help, and (2) what you are willing to do to help solve the problem. Write until you feel as though you are comfortable addressing your problem and turning, in your unsent letter, to him or her for assistance.

Nudge 2

Since this process is not easy, take a moment to congratulate yourself for sticking with it. Write a letter to yourself, explaining how proud you are to be working toward a better, stronger you. Periodically measuring and realizing your progress will give you the boost you need to continue doing this work. It will remind you that you are building tools and honing talents that will carry you safely over the rough waters of life.

CHAPTER THREE

Chipping Away at Anger

*"Wherever passion exists, the energy for transformation
exists, too."*
—Janice Emily Bowers, *A Full Life in a Small Place*

When was the last time you felt anger well up inside of you?
Was it directed toward yourself, another person, or an
event? How long did you remain angry, and how did you act
because you felt this way? Do you often feel angry? Do you know
anyone who seems constantly upset and hostile? What part does
anger play in your life—a huge, defining part or a small, insignificant part?

These days, with life lived fast, faster, and fastest, it seems as
though something upsetting lurks around every corner. Your land-
lord won't fix a broken window, and snow is collecting on your
windowsill. Your child sasses the driver, loses his privilege to take
the bus, and now you must drive him across town to school for a
week. Your boss treats the report you've worked on for a month
as if it were lint on his navy blue sport coat. Your mother won't
stop talking long enough to listen to your concerns about the
cracks appearing in your marriage. You are late for a date, stop to
use an ATM, and the machine eats your credit card.

Life is full of incidents like these, happenings that cause your
jaw to set, stomach to flip-flop, heart to beat faster, muscles to
tighten. The puzzle is figuring out what to do when negative

emotions crop up like knee-jerk responses to the quirks of life. Is it best to bury the anger, hurt, and resentment? To pretend as though the bothersome things in life do not happen or that they do not make our blood boil? Not necessarily. When intense emotions are swallowed, they can simmer below the surface and, at some unpredictable time, explode forth in an unexpected and often surprising emotional outpouring. We act out over something that does not warrant a vehement response and wonder why we have done so while the real source of the anger still hides deep inside.

On the other hand, lashing out is not necessarily the best reaction to the glitches in life either. What good does it do to scream and swear at a waiter who brings you the wrong wine? Or at the dry cleaner who gives you back a dress shirt with more spots on it than when you brought it in, claiming that this is your problem, not hers? Or at your child who moves like molasses while getting ready for school every morning? Getting angry doesn't accomplish what you hope to happen with the situation. So, what are you to do with your anger?

First, it is helpful to know that feeling anger is not the problem. When we experience this emotion, we are being warned that something is calling for our attention. Something or someone is pushing us or someone we love out of our comfort or safety zone. For instance, when someone swerves into our lane on the freeway, we experience anger because we are put in harm's way. When someone breaks into our home, we feel angry because our security has been shattered. When a friend lies to us, we become angry because a trust has been broken. Feeling anger is appropriate and even useful, for it sends a signal we need to hear.

The problem arises when we either feel angry too often or hold on to anger and let it seethe inside for too long so that the emotion begins to affect our health and happiness. "Poorly managed anger is at the root of many serious physical, social and emotional problems, from heart disease to neighborhood violence," said Suzanne Stutman, president of the Institute for Mental Health Initiatives. "By teaching people skills to manage their anger constructively, we empower them with the ability to understand their own and others' feelings and resolve conflict in a nonviolent manner."

During one of the most trying presidential periods in our country's history, Abraham Lincoln had his own way of dealing with anger when it surfaced, a technique that helped him keep the emotion from turning into resentment. In his book *Lincoln on Leadership*, Donald T. Phillips relates that "though once in a while he would blow up and lose his temper, Lincoln usually did it in private. To avoid such a display, Lincoln would sit down and write lengthy letters that he generally did not send. They served as ways to release his pent-up emotional feelings."

There are records that Lincoln often wrote scathing letters and then addressed the envelope, for instance, "To Gen. Meade, never sent, or signed." Phillips tells us that Lincoln said of his unsent letter writing, "I was in such deep distress myself that I could not restrain some expression of it." But the president was wise enough to know when to send his letters and when not doing so would be the more effective choice. He simply wrote his angry letter, filed it away, and went on with his business in a better frame of mind.

Anger happens to the best of us. Who of us has not felt angry within the last week or, perhaps, within the last twenty-four hours? We feel it bubble up inside like an involuntary reflex when something frustrates or threatens us. We respond by giving personal meaning to the experience. A Little Leaguer hits a fly ball through our picture window and what happens next? We begin to use our own set of words to describe the mishap. Some of us might smile and shake our heads, remembering the day when we did the same thing as a youngster. Some of us might jump from our chair, fly to the window, and scream at the youngsters outside. Mark Twain suggested, "When angry, count to four; when very angry, swear. . . ." Some might call the police. Some might turn anger inward, ranting and raving silently about the stupidity of buying a house next to a vacant lot where children gather to play. The truth is that you can take just about any situation and imagine countless emotional responses that might result from it. The reason? The response is not a given. It is a personal assessment of the event. It is the story we choose to tell ourselves about what has happened to us.

Blame accompanies anger like hot fudge keeps company with ice cream. "She made me angry today when she lied to me," we say. "He made me angry when he slammed the door in my face." But does someone have this sort of power over you? Can someone else make you angry any more than they can make you feel love, loneliness, elation, uncertainty, or depression? Not really. We write the emotion into our spirit when we put words to an event. Take, for instance, a day not long ago when I agreed to photograph a group of people on horseback. It wasn't an unreasonable thing to agree to since photography is part of my background. I've made fairly acceptable photographs of people, places, and things for years. So I packed up several cameras and a bag full of film, drove to the stable, and proceeded to take about one hundred shots of the men and women alone, in couples, on their horses, beside their horses, saying good-bye to their horses. In the process some of the cameras broke down. Many of the horses didn't smile. Some of the people inadvertently blocked my view of others in the lineup. And none of the photos matched the perfect group portrait we'd all hoped for and expected. Guess what I did in response? I became angry with myself. "You are dumber than mud," I muttered internally. "Why in the world did you think you could do this job?" I mentally added up the time and money these people had wasted on the photo shoot because they had trusted my talents. "Just think how stupid you're going to feel when you see these people again," I said to myself. "What do they think of you now after this fiasco, you noodle brain?"

Well, I went on and on like this for some time—for too long, actually. My anger had a grip on me. The story I'd written in my head about this incident was planted there as if carved on a gravestone. And don't we do this sort of thing to ourselves all the time? Something happens to us, we respond with our own definition of the event, and we live with it as if that's that, done deal, end of story, we can't go back. Except that we can go back. We do not need to give in to the anger and its residual effects forever. We do not need to accept our anger as if it were a prison from which we cannot escape. The story that came into being when our anger emerged was written by us and can be rewritten within minutes in terms that better suit us. When we take time to diffuse the pent-up anger in our spirits, as did Abraham Lincoln, we gain a better sense of how we choose to react to life and whether our choice of reaction is working for or against us.

Consider the Indian fable about the blind preachers and scholars who were asked to describe an elephant. One, who felt the animal's head, said, "Sire, an elephant is like a pot." Another, who had touched the ear, replied, "An elephant is like a winnowing basket." The one who had observed only a tusk said the animal was a plowshare. The one who had felt its foot said the animal was like a pillar. Each was convinced that he was correct with his definition of the animal. Each maintained a reality based on his limited experience and the words given to that observation.

When we view an experience and the emotions we attach to it from one point of view, we act like the blind men who each insisted that the elephant was exactly as he observed it. Isn't it healthier and wiser to walk around the perimeter of our life events and to rewrite our internal script when our old dialogue hems us in with its narrowness and brings us only pain and sadness? When I didn't produce the photographs I'd hoped to at the horse stable, what did it serve me to berate myself for longer than a moment or, for that matter, for even one moment? My negative assessment of the event didn't help me to learn something new. It didn't inspire me to be my best during the rest of the day. Instead, it pulled me down and kept me low until I was able to crawl out of the doldrums by writing about the event.

What emerged as I let the words flow onto paper in a letter to myself was humor. Who wouldn't laugh at the vision of a "professional" photographer renting a camera with bounce flash, spending an hour at the shop learning how the complicated machine worked, and realizing during the shoot that she'd not asked how to rewind the film? Who wouldn't chuckle at the sight of this "photographer" asking one of the horsemen to please lean forward so she could compose the perfect group photo, then learning that the fellow's bad hips barely allowed him to mount the horse in the first place no less lean forward in the saddle? Who wouldn't grin wide at the vision of this person viewing the prints to see that while she was photographing the horsemen some of the horsemen were photographing one another? I could go on with the humor that I later discovered in the day. But the point is, distance and writing helped me to re-create the story of the event and to shift my emotions from anger toward myself to the healthier, happier response of laughter over life's whimsical nature.

"An angry man is full of poison."
—Confucius

Wanting to be happier and more peaceful is not the only reason to rethink the amount of anger we let into our lives. Medical research has shown that poor management of this emotion is tied to heart disease, some cancers, aggression, and violence. Medical research has also shown that writing is one of the tools we can use to defuse the anger that resides within us. In 1996 in the *Journal of Counseling and Development*, it was reported that, "Properly framed, writing is thought to assuage obsessive internal rumination and continued negative emotions that can exacerbate health and psychological problems." In scientific studies, writing has been shown to alleviate symptoms of asthma and rheumatoid arthritis and to increase the level of disease-fighting lymphocytes in the bloodstream. After extensive research in the field of expressive writing, James Pennebaker, psychology professor at the University of Texas at Austin adds, "Being able to put experiences into words is good for your physical health."

What we believe to be real is the collection of stories we tell ourselves about what is occurring around us. We see. We interpret. We compose a mental or oral tale about what has happened. But the action does not stop there. We either carry the story we have composed inside of us, insisting that what we feel is true, or, we rethink the event by viewing it from more than one angle, then rewrite the script in order to throw off negative thoughts and feelings and to gain greater peace and happiness. The anger is ours. The choice is ours. We can either harbor anger like an old sport coat that doesn't fit any longer and clinches our chest like a wooly vice, or we can say to the anger, "Living with you doesn't suit me well. I've looked at you, through you, under and around you. I've seen you for what you are. And there's no more room in my life for you. Get out."

> *"Anger is a momentary madness, so control your passion or it will control you."*
> —Horace

Even as I write this chapter, my daughter calls from Chicago to tell me that, for a second time in six months, her parked car has been bashed into useless condition by a hit-and-run driver. I think about my suggestion in this book that it is better for us to write ourselves out of anger than to remain held by the emotion. I need to take a dose of my own advice, but I wonder how I can shed the anger I feel. How can I not be angry at the cruel people who have caused my daughter sadness, inconvenience, and costly property injury? How can I not feel angry about the segment of our population that lacks all sense of responsibility for their actions?

The incident reminds me that no matter how much we work at being our emotional best, no matter how much we attempt to bend like a willow when storms blow into our lives, storms happen. They are as much a part of life as peaceful days. Storms happen and I believe that taking time to write about them is better than either remaining silent or acting out. It's not that I can wipe away the emotions I feel at the moment, but writing allows me to feel as though I am doing something in a situation in which I feel totally helpless. It allows me to rant and rave, to scream and shout in my own private way. Writing lets the steam escape and meanwhile reminds me that when life takes us to places beyond our understanding, it's not the storm that is important but how we weather it that makes the difference.

Exercise: Measure Your Anger, Then Bridle It

"An adventure is going into the unknown. . . . Because they involve the unknown, adventures are inherently dangerous to a greater or lesser degree. Yet it is also only from adventures and their newness that we learn. If we know exactly where we're going, exactly how to get there, and exactly what we'll see along the way, we won't learn anything."
—M. Scott Peck, *In Search of Stones: A Pilgrimage of Faith, Reason, and Discovery*

The ultimate goal in writing letters to events that made you angry is not to feel angry all over again, although you will probably do so in the process of diving into the emotion, grabbing hold of it, and writing to it. Rather, the goal of this exercise is to diffuse anger by giving it new names. By dealing with and gaining the upper hand with anger that you harbor over past experiences, it is likely that you will formulate new ways of viewing the emotion and dealing more effectively with it as it happens. We cannot control the events that blow into our lives and that cause us to experience anger, but we can work toward controlling our responses.

In this exercise you will write letters about your anger. As you write you will sort through the clutter of emotions that fills your head and heart. You will examine your emotions carefully and gain new perspective on your troubling thoughts and feelings. Your insight concerning the way you feel about stressful events in your life will deepen, and your ability to react in more effective ways to stressful, threatening events will grow.

As you write letters to your anger, the emotion will shift from being a huge monster that controls and confuses you into being a personal reaction that you can effectively control. The knowledge and insight that you gain through writing letters to or about your anger will empower you to move beyond it, rather than remaining stuck in it. As Jon Kabat-Zinn says in his book *Wherever You Go There You Are*, "Awareness sees the anger; it knows the depth of the anger, and it is larger than the anger." Taking a close look at your anger may take you places you've never visited before, but doing so gives you the opportunity to gain control over this ungainly emotion.

Nudge 1

To begin the process of taking stock of your anger, write a letter to yourself about the role anger plays in your life. List the first five angry situations that come to mind. Explain what it was that angered you and how you reacted to each event. Describe how long you remained angry in each instance and what the anger did to your frame of mind, to your ability to effectively function during the rest of that day or that week, and to your ability to deal with the people in your life. If you can think of further events that angered you, keep writing until you run out of examples. You may need to return to this exercise several times to address every incident that you can think of that caused your anger to flare. Being thorough with this exercise will provide you an in-depth look at how you react to and deal with stressful events and how anger affects your life.

Nudge 2

Now that you have painted a thorough word portrait of anger as it appears in your life today, go back to your childhood and write about several events that angered you then. Think of two, three, or four memories of being angry, and write about the situations that caused your strong reaction. As you write, consider the following words to see whether any are better than anger to describe how you felt: rage, fury, dismay, indignation, wrath, ire, embitterment, enmity, illwill, horror, frustration, terror, panic, confusion.

Compare your childhood reactions to the upsetting event to your reactions today when something similar happens. How is your anger different today than it was years ago? Why do you think you act similarly or differently as an adult? Continue to write about your anger as a child until you feel as though you have discovered something about yourself by doing so. Describe what you have learned, and then move on to the next nudge.

Nudge 3

> *"If you are patient in one moment of anger, you will escape a hundred days of sorrow."*
> —Chinese proverb

Since the majority of our experiences with anger are connected to everyday irritations, you will write to one of these insignificant events before addressing a major one. Choose one of the smaller incidents you mentioned in your "taking stock" letters, then think of yourself as a prehistoric man or woman who believes that drawing a stick figure on a cave wall holds magic power. At the top of your page, draw a simple figure that symbolizes the anger you feel over the experience you have chosen to write about. Your symbol may be a black cloud, a thorn, a vulture, a bolt of lightning. Have fun with the selection of your symbol of anger.

Now write to this figure, explaining how much larger you are than it. Explain how this anger once had control over you, causing you distress. Explain that now you are gaining control over your anger by drawing it and writing to it. Tell this symbol that you are shifting the power back into your own hands and will no longer be subject to the whim of anger.

Using a simple drawing as a symbol of your anger will help you break out of your usual mode of thinking so you can begin to see with new eyes and write new stories for yourself. Approaching your writing in this fashion is like the use of puppets in child psychology. When children speak to a puppet about feelings and experiences, they tend to be much less reserved than when speaking to a counselor directly. Imagination helps them get beyond the rules of behavior that block their ability to be totally honest and open. In the same way, you can pretend your way into discovery by addressing an object such as a crow circling in the sky; a thorn-covered cactus; a big, black bear; or a long and lonely downtown street at dawn.

In your letter be sure to explain what the stressful event and resulting anger have done to your well-being, your strength and health, and your ability to relate to others and to accomplish your work. Describe what you would like to do to and with this emotion. Explain why you selected the animal or object you chose to symbolize your anger. Imagine that in the act of writing you are magically casting a spell over the symbol so that you become its master and keeper.

Try to let go with this exercise. Be a child. Pretend your pen has a life of its own and you are there, just observing the words and ideas as they appear on the paper. Write for twenty minutes or more without stopping, without censoring yourself.

Nudge 4

Before you write your next letter, take a moment to consider the fact that trees, flowers, and animals have long been symbols of mysticism and magic, each with its own characteristics and qualities, each with its own lessons to teach. Your choice of a symbol for your anger may have a great deal to teach you. Think about the symbol you chose. Consider its form, color, voice, movement, and relationship to others of its species. Listen to your symbol as it writes to you and through you in the following letter.

Now pretend you are the imaginary object or animal to whom you just wrote. If it helps you to get into the other's frame of mind, change the writing utensil and the type of paper you are using. Sit in a different chair or a different room. Write with your other hand or stop using punctuation. Be creative in putting on the other's hat as you write a letter back to yourself in the other's voice. As you write from this different perspective, allow the emotion personified by the object or animal to have its say to you—the person who has been under anger's spell for a while. Perhaps the object or animal will want to give *you* a new name. Perhaps it will make suggestions to you about your behavior. Perhaps it will try to make you even angrier than you were before. Once again, let your words melt onto the paper. After you shift your mind into the character of the anger, do not censor what the emotion wants to tell you. Let it speak to you.

Keep the dialogue going back and forth between yourself and the anger until you feel as though you have gained greater understanding about the true nature of anger, about how it arises and how it works either for or against you, and about how you can handle anger in the future and, perhaps, use it for your benefit rather than your detriment.

Nudge 5

Now choose a more significant event that caused you to feel angry in the past and/or causes you anger currently. Write a letter to the person or thing that was central to the event. Write for at least twenty minutes without pausing or censoring, pouring out your thoughts and feelings as if pouring your emotion out of a bottomless pitcher. Let it flow. Feel the emotion seeping through your fingers, through the pen, into words on the paper.

As you write your letters about anger, you might want to slip into your age when the troublesome event occurred. If you were four years old, try to talk as if you were four, using simple language and referring to people and objects as you might have when very young. Write your letter with a crayon or fat, yellow pencil. See what you learn by experimenting with this shift in years. As you write additional letters to the person or thing that caused you anger, compose them as though you are growing older. Watch your insight broaden and mature.

SAMPLE LETTER: FROM LOIS GREENE STONE, PITTSFORD, NEW YORK, WRITTEN AS AN UNSENT LETTER, BUT EVENTUALLY MAILED.

Cope! I want to shout this command to you, my married daughter, the same way I used to order you to stop whining or teasing your brothers. At the same time, a part of me wants to soothe, but I seem to repress that desire.

So you're forced to move because of your husband's job, and phone me with "familiar," and "been here eight years" and "don't want to be uprooted."

I've attempted to tread that fine line between reassurance and sympathy but my feet slip from the guide wire and I sound indifferent. Sensing your pain, I still blurt out callous sentences like, "Your husband didn't expect the company he worked for to fold. Be glad he's wanted somewhere using his training. It's not forever." I certainly didn't hear this kind of talk from my own widow-mother; she was so sensitive to me and everyone.

I know on the phone I've said: "Stop whining! It's not that bad. You'll be in a safer community. Your kids will know seasons out of the tropical climate. Maybe, with seasons, you'll be aware of time passing and appreciate it." Why am I reprimanding? Why a lecture when I hated being talked to this way while growing up? Why haven't I become more like my mother?

Pebble by pebble, I seem to have started a rocky wall between my house and your apartment. If I speak a stone gets added, if I don't speak a stone gets added. Am I reliving my own fears when I was forced to move five different times during the first seven years of marriage? But you are spunkier than I was, more adequate, and I thought you knew about your inner strength.

"Grandma. I'm going to move. It sometimes snows there. I'm going to learn to skate, and take my sister on a sled, and catch snow with my tongue." Your small son told me this, so how do you transmit so much positive to both of your children yet have tunnel vision for yourself? I am trying to understand your anger; maybe these phone calls are your way of just wanting to cry "Mom . . . kiss and make better" because you're tired of being grown-up all the time. My mother would have known this automatically; I'm still learning.

Movers did what movers sometimes do: came at the wrong time, didn't bring enough packing boxes, disassembled furniture that was never intended to be taken apart, had a truck too small and had to stuff items under its belly and ride some on the roof. You said you all slept on a bare floor that night.

I know I mumbled words of optimism, but sounded irritated. You screamed at me, drowning, wanting me to send a life preserver of unconditional love and just ears to listen; I sent enthusiasm and a "don't worry about your furniture in advance" morality.

Then your foreboding became reality as almost all your belongings were damaged, some boxes lost, precious handmade possessions broken. Maintenance workers for your rental space hadn't come to fix broken plumbing, inadequate air circulation vents, and so forth. And with more of your frantic calls, I carried my response—a mixture of emotional support and I-can't-listen-anymore.

But I whispered to the telephone receiver, once back in its cradle: Cope, darling. Don't fall apart . . . but only the silence heard me.

And now, with some time that's passed, and with the same feisty independence and capability you display most of the time, of course you adjusted, adapted, created a comfortable atmosphere for your family. And you're so much like my own mother since you've left the imaginary fence of pebbles behind and probably never will bring them up. For that, I'm grateful. My mother used to say she learned from her children. I thought she was being patronizing as I struggled to explode the "me" into a separate entity. I'm now aware her wisdom sneaks in, influences me, and I wish she were alive so I could tell her.

I'm attempting to learn how to release my inner desires to soothe you and your brothers, since you're all adults, and to appreciate the tenacity of you three. If an overwhelming boo-boo needs a Band-Aid of compassion, I'll try taping it with respect for your honesty and courage to cry. Cope. You certainly confront life's turmoil as well as its tribulation; I'm learning from you.

Next write back to yourself from the viewpoint of the person or event you have addressed in your letter. Try not to interfere with the voice of the writer. Let it have its way on paper, for you will be given rebuttal time with the next letter you write, from your own point of view. Once again, write back and forth between yourself and the person or event until insight happens. Writing your letters first from your own and then from someone else's point of view forces you to creatively broaden your appreciation of the total situation. It's all in what you think, so think creatively in this exercise and get a handle on the anger that has been keeping you from feeling your absolute best. In reality we can never walk in the shoes of another. But by using your imagination, you will gradually get deeper inside of your own heart by pretending that you are able to crawl inside that of another person and his or her point of view.

Nudge 6

You have been using the nudges in this exercise to write letters to
an object, event, or person other than yourself. Now it's time to
address the anger you feel toward your own imperfections. We
are not perfect beings. We do wrong against ourselves and others.
It's our tendency to cling to the memory of our mistakes and to
hate the part of ourselves that failed to be perfect. This anger,
like any other, does nothing but drag us down.

Make a list of the mistakes you have made in your life that
cause you anger. Choose one of these and write a letter to yourself
from today's viewpoint. What would you do differently now than
you did when you made the mistake? What new information do
you have today that would enable you to make this better choice?
Describe yourself as you were when you made the mistake, taking
into consideration your age, your maturity level, the things you
did not know at the time. The moment you made the mistake was
not the whole story. Now, you can look back on the situation and
make note of the details you were unaware of then but see now—
details that enable you to understand why you did what you have
considered a mistake.

Love yourself as you write this letter. Be your best friend, not
your fiercest critic. Be as understanding and accepting with the
part of you that failed to be perfect as you would with your dearest
friend or with your son or daughter. The object of this exercise
is to cure the wounds in your heart and to feel good about yourself
as an imperfect, but quite lovable, person.

Come back to this exercise until you have addressed all of the
areas of hurt against yourself. Come back to this exercise until
you have looked at each situation that once caused you anger
about your past, have examined each from every possible angle,

and can move forward feeling that you love and accept yourself today and yesterday.

Nudge 7

Keep writing letters to and from the many sources of your anger until you feel that you have the upper hand with your anger rather than it having control over you. In your final letter for this chapter, describe your joy and relief with finally becoming stronger than your anger. Describe how it feels to have accomplished this task. Congratulate yourself on your hard work and new awareness. Explain how you plan to use this awareness to deal with anger when it surfaces in the future.

SAMPLE LETTER: FROM BECKIE A. MILLER, GLENDALE, ARIZONA, WRITTEN TO A DECEASED SON AFTER LOSING HIM TO MURDER. "WRITING ALLOWS ME TO SING MY SON'S SILENCED SONG," SHE SAYS.

Dearest Brian,

It has now been over five years since you were torn from our lives by the senseless greed of another, your same age. I resent the passage of time, as it mocks my grief with daring to move forward. I have survived and gone on to give meaning to the pain that endures forever, and yet, my heart is always half-mast without you.

I resent the emotional energy that I expend in attempting to get the one who shot you to death for your wallet, in prison for murder. He is only serving seven years for aggravated robbery, due to a plea agreement given him wrongfully. I want to forget him. It is hard enough living without you. There is so little energy left for him. Yet I must. If I do not try, a cold-blooded murderer will walk the streets again, as you did that fateful morning, in his path and the path of two bullets marked for you.

This year you would have been twenty-four years old. You would undoubtedly be married with children of your own. You were so good with kids. My last memory of you, the day before you were killed, is of you cradling two-month-old Tracey in your arms, cooing to her, attempting to coax a smile from her colic fussiness, while I tended to others in my home day care. I thank God for that special moment. We could have been arguing about your quitting some of your college classes. We could have been arguing about the usual things a mom and son argue about when she realizes her son is growing away from her into his own. I am so grateful the last few minutes I was allowed to share with you were tender.

It is hard to see your friends, grown and married, having children. My heart is happy for their gain but crying for what I will never share with you, what we were robbed of, too. Your sister has had such a hard time dealing with the pain, the anger, and the fear. A fourteen-year-old when you were killed, not capable of accepting the horror of learning of her own mortality through yours and that another can take a life so easily, so cruelly. Missing her brother, her only sibling, learning life does indeed go on and wondering, as I do, how it can. I know you walk each step of her journey alongside her, as with us. I am comforted by that fact, and still we miss you more than words can ever truly express.

Your father lost not only you, an extension of himself, but the last bearer of his family name. You were the only male to carry on the tradition of countless generations. Gone, lost forever. His grief is different than mine, intermingled with rage, powerlessness. A father, a man, always wants to be his family's protector from all harm. He could not save you from another. It burns in him, the cruel unfairness of it all. If you could see his gentleness, his joy, with the new baby we adopted, the sister who will never know you, you would know he will be OK. His demons of grief will diminish in time. The anger will slowly burn away with the cleansing of healing tears.

We owe it to ourselves and to your memory to go on. To forge ahead and live and laugh again. It would have been so tempting to allow the heavy burden of sorrowful grief drown us. It would have been easy to give in to the darkness, the void of living without joy. So much of our joy was taken that it amazes me there is any left. Your new sister showed us there was. She breathes so much happiness and life back into this family with a missing piece.

I never thought I could experience absolute joy again, once you were ripped from my heart. I did, and I realized you gave me permission. I hear it whispered in the wind blowing through the branches of the tree planted in your memory—Brian's Tree. I hear it in the memories of who you were in life, warm, compassionate, and serious. I hear it in my heart and from above. I know it is right and honorable to take a mother's love, through grief, and wrap it as a precious gift around another. You would have loved your new sister dearly, as your first sister.

Dearest son, who once gave me the meaning of life, now I give life the meaning of you in honoring your memory with truly living again, despite the endless pain. I thank God for the eighteen years we shared together. It should have been more and in many ways it is. Thank you dearest one.

Love always, Mom, Dad and your Sisters

CHAPTER FOUR

Romancing the Special People in Your Life

"What is this thing called love?
This funny thing called love?
Just who can solve its mystery?
Why should it make a fool of me?"
    —From Cole Porter's "What Is This Thing Called Love?"

Is there anything in life as complicated, wild, and wonderful as love? Is there anything that demands as much work, perseverance, and commitment? As much patience, understanding, and sacrifice?

There's no doubt that our relationships give life meaning. We bond with one another in a natural process, thereby enriching our days and avoiding a life of solitude. We meet fascinating people and fall in love with the unique visions, attitudes, and life experiences they bring to us. We form immediate and extended families and turn to one another for support, meaning, respect, love, and understanding. And then time and change happen. Our connections become more complicated. Relationships shift and grow more complex with history. Friendships open into intricate blossoms that need tending or wither away from neglect or disinterest. Moments of ecstasy with the people we love couple with times of disagreement, disappointment, and ultimately great sadness when dear family members, friends, teachers, mentors, pets, and lovers die.

"The source of one's joy is also the source of one's sorrow."
—Jessamyn West

There is nothing like love, nothing like the pleasure and richness of a relationship that lasts for a glowing month or an entire lifetime. But one day you are the best spouse in the world; the next day you drive your partner to distraction. On Monday your child votes you parent of the year and by Friday that same child wants to run away and never see you again. In January your best friend tells you she cannot imagine what she would do without you, and by May she has moved away, forgotten your phone number, and fallen out of communication.

Relationships are like that. They just don't stay the same. We mature, find new interests, direct our attention first this way, then that. The unexpected happens and we act in unexpected and unplanned ways. Change is the only constant we can count on for certain in our relationships—oh, yes, and the need for work. Falling in love is easy. We would like the fun and good times to continue forever. But relationships cannot thrive and grow any more than our African violet would last without constant attention, patience, warmth, understanding, and care.

". . . since it requires the extension of ourselves, love is always either work or courage. There are no exceptions."
—M. Scott Peck, *The Road Less Traveled*

Over the years I've gone in and out of understanding what it means to be a daughter, sister, wife, mother to a son and a daughter, daughter-in-law, business partner, neighbor, and friend. When wearing any one of these hats became confusing, writing a letter was my way out of the fog. Sometimes, after writing and rewriting from one end of my confusion to the other, I would deliver a "final," polished letter to the person on the other side of my struggle. I can still see the look on my son's face as he would walk out of his bedroom holding one such letter I'd left on his desk. He'd be thinking, "Here she goes again." But I'd be thinking, "Whatever happens now, at least I took the time to get clear about my feelings concerning this issue and have said what I needed to say as best I could."

At this point the mist of my confusion would have evaporated through the process of writing and rewriting letters to myself and, then, to my son. I could listen to my son's response more effectively than I could have before examining my thoughts and feelings on paper. Invariably, the discussion that followed was less emotional or bothersome than I had expected. I imagine this was true because my cards were face up on the table. My son had seen them and knew I was keeping nothing up my sleeve as he placed his cards next to mine. As much as he dreaded getting these letters, the rules were understood. He knew that my letters came only after great thought. And I believe he knew that they were written with great love and care.

Sometimes, I would deliver such a final letter to a family member or friend. But often the writing was for me. Just yesterday I found a letter I'd written to my daughter several years ago. It was still in the sealed, addressed, stamped envelope. It was in my file drawer, not in her heart. The troubles I worked through in that letter were mine. I had helped myself grow through and beyond an emotional speed bump by writing that letter. I believe that sending the thoughts contained in my unsent message would have worked like dumping a bucket of ice water onto our relationship. In this case the problem resided in my bank of thoughts, beliefs, attitudes, and experiences. I desired to wrestle with the feelings that were gumming up my mental workings, but that did not mean Kristi needed or wanted to walk through the muck with me. At times having my child, friend, parent, or husband join me in the sticky process only confounds my issue. So I go it alone, in quiet, in writing—and the end result is a new awareness and peacefulness that I can take with me when I once again face those whom I dearly love.

We can work through our confusion about a relationship by writing letters that we do not intend to send. But consider the many other ways we can keep love alive by writing letters. We can profess our love, nurture it, define and repair it. We can prevent clashes by taking the fuse out of anger in letters written but not sent. We can preserve love by clarifying for ourselves what we need in our relationship and by clarifying, as well, what we are willing to offer to the other person in the relationship. We can honor love by defining how much the special people in our lives mean to us. While spoken words evaporate, written words remain to heal, to seal a bond, to warm the heart on a cold and windy night. By writing letters that you do not send, you work toward eventually writing a letter that effectively strengthens and improves the love in your life.

Exercise: Explore the Valleys and Peaks of Love

In preparation for the following exercises, consider the many types of love that you have felt in your life: the immeasurable love for a newborn child; the passionate love for a new beau; the gentle love for an aged relative; the tested love for an old friend; the grateful love for a physician, counselor, or clergyman; the proven love for a spouse of forty years; the broken love of a relationship that did not last; the mended love of a relationship that fell apart and was gently pieced back into being; the love of a pet, a home or homeland, a neighborhood.

Now consider the many people in your life for whom you feel love. Think about all of the people in the past who have brought color, joy, and learning into your life, like your first sweetheart, your first best friend, your first-grade teacher, your relatives who are no longer with you. Consider all of the people who currently make your life richer and fuller, like your spouse, friends, parents, children, teachers, doctors, co-workers, bosses, and neighbors. Your biggest challenge may be choosing which person you will write to in your first unsent letter for this exercise.

The type of message you write today could be a letter of regret, explaining the hurt caused by a breakup that happened years ago or yesterday. It could be a letter of sadness because your current relationship is not as deep as you wish it to be. It could be a letter of disappointment to your child, explaining the aspect of your relationship that does not match your expectation. Or, it might be a request to yourself that you learn to accept those parts of your personality that feel foreign or frightening. You could write to yourself if you have lost affection for yourself or if you feel as though a part of you has grown unlikable. Accepting yourself, warts and all, is just as important as accepting the humanness of everyone else in your life.

No matter who you write to or what the focus of your letter, the objective of doing the following exercises is to expand your understanding of your relationships by looking at them as you would an intricate painting. It is impossible to understand any work of art without examining the medium and how it was used, the subject matter and how it was treated, the visual details and how they relate to one another. Those who study art investigate the artist's life, his body of work, and the influences that affected his work.

In the same way, we cannot grasp the whole of our relationships without looking at many of the countless moments that came together to create the whole. Creating your lists and writing your unsent letters will force you to explore your relationship from many angles, from the peaks, valleys, and level land in between. This exercise will help you remember aspects of your relationship that might have been forgotten in the busyness of living. You may even smile to yourself as you remember moments or events that you have not thought about for a long, long time. Or, a new flood of tears may well up from inside as you mentally relive a hurtful moment whose embers still burn in your heart.

SAMPLE LETTER: FROM MARIL CRABTREE,
KANSAS CITY, MISSOURI.
My dear husband,

You are my tropical island and my ocean breeze, my mountain retreat and my big-city hideaway. You are my heart beating in the middle of the night and a tangle of my hair blowing in the wind.

You've loved me longer than I've loved myself, and deeper. When I look into your eyes, I come home to something I never even knew I missed, and I breathe a prayer of thanks for the wrinkles around those eyes, for the slightly stooped shoulder I sleep on, for the extra folds of waistline I lean against when we dance.

There were years when my love for you slowed to a trickle; your love for me was as constant as a waterfall. And I finally understood that your love, this great, wonderful, never-ending love, is unconditional. It doesn't depend on what I do or don't do, how I look or what I say. It just is. Like islands and oceans and mountains just are. And still we dance, into the next day, into the next millennium, God willing, and always into each other's hearts.

All around us are couples who break up for some reason or other, and I used to think that someday it might happen to us. But you say we are soul mates, and it simply can't happen. And I believe you because it makes me happier than listening to my own dry-desert doubts. Neither your belief nor my doubts have any rational basis, so why not choose to believe in love? The Pascalian wager, Kirkegaard's leap of faith: We love, you and I, because we choose to love. You show me every day what is possible when the two of us choose to love and to share that love with the rest of the world. For that gift, I am willing to take a lifetime's worth of soul, and know that I can't lose.

Nudge 1

Choose one person from the many in your life for whom you feel love. Then, finish each of the following phrases with at least ten thoughts that come to mind about that person. Don't stop at ten if there are one hundred things you can list.

- "I love (or loved) you because. . . ."

- "I wish we could (or would have) . . ." and/or "I regret that we. . . ."
- "We were good for one another when (or because) we. . . ."
- "The relationship didn't work (or isn't working as I'd like it to) for us because. . . ."
- "Our most ecstatic moments together occurred when . . ." and, "Our lowest, most difficult times together are (or were) when. . . ."

Feel free to create your own titles for these or additional lists. Take your time with this nudge. Reach deep inside for your responses. If one simple sentence is not enough for a response, write more. These lists, and the thought you put into them, will be sparks that ignite letters for following exercises and perhaps for years to come. List making has a way of scratching through the surface to thoughts, feelings, and memories that have been in hiding. So have fun with these lists, pour your heart into them, and see where they take you.

Nudge 2

Once your lists are complete, choose one negative or bothersome item from the responses that flowed onto your page to be the focus of your first letter. Write an unsent letter today to your lover, friend, relative, or yourself about this bothersome aspect of your relationship.

In your letter describe where the uneven terrain exists in your relationship. Be specific as you write. Generalities will keep the waters muddy; specifics will dig down to the roots of the problem. Read love poems for inspiration. Pretend you are painting a picture of the problems that exist between you and someone important in your life, and describe your painting. Pretend that you and the person to whom you write are two different types of animals trying to learn to coexist. The purpose of pretending to look through the eyes of an artist, an animal, a seer, or the wallpaper in your living room is to break out of old ways of seeing your relationship. Experiment as you write your letter. Pretend, write, dream, and scheme until you discover possibilities for new, refreshing ways of seeing your relationship and of being together in this world.

SAMPLE LETTER: FROM L.G. HUNT, ARLINGTON, VIRGINIA.

Dear Valentine,

When I got up this morning, leaving you snoring in our bed, I came downstairs hoping for roses and chocolate truffles, a diamond bracelet, and opera tickets. Or even a single daisy and a homemade card with red paper hearts cut out of a magazine. Instead I found a sink full of dirty dishes left from last night.

I wasn't surprised. The only thing that surprises me is how I continue to hope that you'll be something I know you aren't. Whose fault is that? Mine, of course. What did I expect after all this time?

Everyone says you're a good person. But they describe you by negatives. He doesn't lie, doesn't cheat. He isn't cruel, isn't hateful. I'd longed for positives, not negatives. He is romantic, is surprising, is filled with joie de vivre. See, I'd even thought of you in French.

In a few minutes I'll wake you, as soon as the coffee's ready, and you'll get up, shower, go off to work. You're reliable. You've always done what you said you were going to do. Exactly. I should have listened more carefully.

Now it's quiet, a gray February morning belonging to the rest of my life. I hear an occasional snore from you, slow rain whispering on the roof. I used to love that sound. It was cozy. Now? Now it says something else to me. Be grateful for a safe life, for modesty and decency. Remember the kidney transplant, the winning lottery ticket you gave to the Salvation Army.

Now I'm going to tear this up, with love.

Nudge 3

Write another unsent letter the next day after you have had time to reflect upon your first message and have read it aloud to yourself. Your feelings are likely to shift and expand from those you expressed yesterday. After all, the way we are with those we love shifts moment by moment like the sands in a dune. So, let your second letter build upon the first. Address the twists and turns of your relationship. Write about the ebb and flow of the happiness, sadness, discovery, confusion, question, and answer of your relationship.

Treat these letters like the chapters of a book, one following and growing out of the letter that went before. You will find that when you are away from your writing, when you are thinking about something else, your mind will continue to process your reactions to what you have said in your letter. New thoughts will pop into your mind that you will be able to focus on in the next letter you write.

Come back to this exercise day after day, writing letter after letter. With each "chapter" you write, you will not only slice a little deeper through the many layers of your feelings, but you will also shed bits and pieces of the discomfort, confusion, or sadness you harbor about the relationship or person.

As you write one letter, then another and another to your friend, relative, associate, lover, or self, pretend that you are walking around the situation and seeing it from the north, south, east, and west. Write about your relationship as if you are seeing it by morning light, at noontime, during dinner, and finally by midnight moonlight. Describe your relationship as if you were walking with it through autumn leaves, through the first snow of winter, through gentle ocean surf.

Remember when you were a child and pretended that you were Superman, a teacher, a cowboy, or an actress? You were playing. You were using your natural, inborn imagination to transport yourself to places and situations that were as real to you as sitting at dinner with your family. For a moment, be a child. Use your imagination to see yourself in your relationship from as many new angles as possible.

By doing this exercise over and again, you will begin to see a pattern emerging. You will begin to grasp a greater understanding of the manner in which you relate to the people in your life. And, you will soothe old wounds that inevitably come with ever-changing human relationships.

SAMPLE LETTER: FROM LIZ CORDONNIER, AVON, CONNECTICUT.

My dearest son,

The other day I watched a woman and her tiny baby boy outside the library. She maneuvered the stroller with care down the wide cement steps, and I appreciated how easy it is for me to get around these days unhampered by such necessities. When the baby started to cry, the mother stopped and sat on the bench beside me. The sound—so helpless, so dependent, so distraught—of the baby who does not have the luxury of words, brought back memories so vivid that I could feel them in my breasts that used to nurture you. The woman picked the baby up, and I remembered when you had those minute, perfect little fingernails. What a miracle they were to me, and your chubby hands with dimples for knuckles.

A smile from his mother and the baby's mercurial mood was gone. Drool clung to his lips and tears to his eyelashes as he returned her smile with his own. I had thought that life was easy because I had dispensed with carriages and cradles. I had forgotten how simple it once was to coo and nuzzle your cheek and make you happy to your very toes. How you lit up when I talked to you, babbling nonsense back to me. How I have to pry words out of you these days in order to connect.

A tough, fearless kid, the only thing that ever frightened you was being alone at night in your room. When I tucked you in, you often begged to be snuggled. Sometimes I would. We'd lay together until your sweet, shallow breaths turned slow and deep. Sometimes I would linger even longer to watch the serenity in your face. I thought that you'd quickly grow out of that desire, but it had to be me to say, "No more. You are a big boy now. Ten is too old to be snuggled by your mom."

I don't tell you, but sometimes I long to ask you for one more snuggle. But that is over. The fence I erected was strong. Eleven years ago, I did not leave you to cry in your crib because I considered it cruel. Today I take the precious money your grandfather has given you because you've lost your jacket. Today I make you refuse invitations to play because you are behind in your homework. The sunshine beckons, and you have been cooped up in your classroom all day. You stomp to your room, and I feel you are justified in hating me. I'd hate me, too. Now when you cry in your room the sound is just as desperate, but I cannot come and comfort you. You do not want me. I do not give in, but I ache for you.

Today your fingernails are as big as mine and embedded with playground dirt. Your sanguine smile is filled with braces. I act like I know, my baby, but I don't always know. It is my job to help you become the best person you can be. Will you forgive me my mistakes some day? Will I forgive myself?

Remember that I love you, Mom

Nudge 4

It is now time to write an unsent letter to your friend, relative, lover, or self about one of the positive elements of your relationship that you listed for Nudge 1 (page 77) of this chapter. No relationship is without both positive and negative elements. The sea does not exist which has only calm or stormy waters. Reminding ourselves, and the most important people in our lives, about the strengths that exist in our relationships is vital to keeping love alive. In relationships, positive magnifies and draws positive to itself. Warmth fills up the cold, empty spaces. Gentleness smoothes a rough spot in a relationship like water softens ragged edges of a boulder it flows over and around.

Take the time today to write a love letter to someone in your life. Set time aside on a regular basis to remind yourself about the special people in your life and to tell these folks how important they are, how they touch your life and make it better. If you wish to send these letters, do so. Then watch as the love returns to you.

SAMPLE LETTER: FROM JAMES MCGRATH, SANTA FE, NEW MEXICO.

Dear old friend Cecile,

I left you standing in your garden of ferns and bougainvillea so long ago. You had made a beautiful lunch of snails in coconut milk and watercress that you had gathered in your garden there in Baguio City, Philippines . . . and banana lumpia with fresh coffee roasted from your own coffee bush beans.

I've carried the sweet taste of coconut milk and honied bananas with me for years. The heavy brown of that coffee returns whenever I sit alone with a cafe latte or espresso. No one has gathered snails in their backyard for me since, nor picked bananas from their trees, nor pulled coffee berries from bushes in their garden and roasted them over coals for grinding and drinking. Your world was magic. It remains a picture of joy and peace. It was a world to be shared, and you shared it with me.

This letter, written so many times in silence, comes to you on a long breath of pleasure and appreciation, filling the years between then and now with love. I know it will be lost in the mails from here to Baguio City. But if the energy of it reaches you in reflective moments between the smell of coffee berries roasting and the gathering of snails, I will be happy. I shall return to your bit of paradise, honey sweet and fragrant, whenever I think of you.

With my love, James

CHAPTER FIVE

Facing Your Grief Head-On

"As the boy had never looked upon the sea, nor any body of water he couldn't see over, he had no word for the landscape that he faced."
  —Wright Morris, *Writing My Life*

A few months ago, I lost my friend Judy to cancer. During her long illness, I felt like the little boy in the quote who lacked words for the vast unknown lying before him. Most days we think we are in control. We pretend to hold the world in the palm of our hands. Then something happens, and we realize how out of control and vulnerable we really are. During her battle with brain tumors, Judy often asked me, "Lauren, what am I supposed to do?" Her mortality stared her in the face and confounded her. She asked medical and spiritual questions for which there were no answers. She was frightened, sad beyond words, and regretful that she could not take charge of her life. Her days were being cut short, and, try as she did until her last breath, she could not change the course of her journey.

I had never before stood by the side and held the hand of a dear friend whose life slipped away visibly like sand through an hourglass. During the last year and a half of Judy's life, I tried to write about my feelings but my fingers, heart, and mind were disconnected. Language refused to make something real of what was happening to my friend and her family.

It wasn't until after Judy died that I was able to begin writing down my feelings about the experience of her illness. The writing started when I agreed to speak at her memorial service. Then, I was forced out of love and obligation to find something to say about what had happened to Judy and, consequentially, to me. It took days to write my good-bye. It took strength I didn't know I had to voice my message to Judy in front of those gathered in her honor. But there was no other way for me to move forward. My time with Judy as I had known it was finished. It was time to begin a new form of communication with her that would soothe my aching heart. To do this I needed to write many letters to her and to read one of them aloud, among those who loved her.

As I wrote to Judy, a vision came to mind of the two of us bicycling through Maine with our husbands years before. Up, down, and around the coastline we peddled for one week. I could see Judy up ahead of me on her bicycle, or in my rearview mirror, as she peddled behind me. We weren't able to talk while on the road. Either breathlessness or distance prevented us from carrying on our usual chatter. But the vision of her there, nearby, huffing and puffing slowly but determinedly to the top of each long upgrade or sailing free as the wind downhill, made my way a bit easier and much more fun than going it alone.

We were separate yet together on that bicycle trip in a way that was similar to our being separate but together during Judy's illness. Sometimes during those many months, the talking was difficult. Sometimes we just held hands as if holding tight to a life raft. When we did talk, we asked questions and searched for answers together, as we always had. We were there for one another in a way that I believe made a difference to both of us.

After Judy died I discovered a comforting way to think about our friendship as I wrote letters to her. The vision of Judy and me bicycling together on the road of life soothes me. I see us continuing the journey side by side, searching together for clarity, inspiring one another to be strong and true. Sometimes I write letters to her, sometimes I talk to her spirit to spirit, sometimes I set words upon the wind in her direction. Even as I write this sentence, I feel her presence as though we are peddling in unison to the top of one more hill.

My connection to Judy, and your connection to the important people in your life, mean so much that saying good-bye is just as important and meaningful as saying hello. Without a good-bye a hole remains in our hearts. The sadness that cries for release after the death of a loved one has no place to rest without a good-bye. Without a good-bye there remains a gnawing discomfort that something has been left undone.

EXTENDED SAMPLE LETTER: FROM CX DILLHUNT, MADISON, WISCONSIN.

August 26, 1997

Dear Mil,

Where do we go? I have a hard time figuring out where you are, other than physically, in my heart. I mean, before you died you weren't. Well, sometimes, in and out, but now I realize we were making the place where I could hold you now. The hole is still there. My heart has just grown bigger, more bearable. If there is a way for you to talk to me, I will listen. If there is a way to go where you are, I will go. Teach me more. Tell me what to say.

Always, Sil

July 21, 1998
Hi Mil,

Just a quick update on the kids, to tell you your newest grandchildren are so beautiful. Mary Jane is almost six months old, and we can hardly wait to see little Nicolas for the first time. Hard to believe that now all your girls have kids. I know how happy you'd be. Today is Kathy's and my twenty-eighth wedding anniversary. I am in constant shock these days. We talk of irritating each other. We miss you so. What I've figured out is the cost of living . . . and that we are all like trees, some taller, some thought to be prettier, some dying. Not to write would be to stop snow in midair, to keep the cicada from its shrill chirping, to stop trees from turning. I am lucky to have lived long enough to have overlapped your life. I read we learn to be kind from the dead.

Love always, Sil

August 11, 1999
Dear Mil,

You must know by now that I'm nearly out of grief, that I cry mostly for fear of running out of words, for fear of running into you, and for the words I have for you. What am I to do when you will not answer, when I grow fond of the silence? What of this endless speaking for two (even when I am silent), which you would tell me is the way it has always been. What am I to do, what am I to say?

You have been dead for three years. I am three years older, but also three years dead, and I don't know what to do with this death of me. It is true that it is less frightening. It is true less is said of you. It is true you never write back. But then where does the confusion come from, where are these words going to? If you return, where will I find you?

And you must know that I worry who will write to you once I am gone. You must know that I am alive, how every word drips with your name. I am afraid to let you die, to let you go where you go. You must know by now.

On the way back from Manistique last week, I realized that the poem is the residue, the poem is not the act. It is not the collection, it is the making itself. But how I wonder what it is we hang on to, where it goes when we let go.

I'm sure you get a chuckle or two knowing that if I'd only settle down, you'd write back, tell me a thing or two. Dear mother-in-law, give me your name for sun, your place for day, the size of what you collect. Tell where we go, where we come back from.

Love always, Sil

December 11, 1999
Dear Mil,

I am amazed we have so much to say to each other, that you are still here. It's as if you'd never left. It's as if I go back to Milwaukee and you are still there. It's three years and four months, but the counting seems so little today. Is there another way to count? How I would die to hear from you, to get a card, a word, a note. Oh, do write, one more time, write all the time, write so loudly, so often that I will no longer be lonely for you, will no longer doubt that you are indeed the house, the words of sunrise, the air, each breath.

I am imagining I know how to read your poetry. I find myself sitting with a book in my hand. A book which is not your poetry, which is not your story but in which you are speaking nonetheless. I sit here imagining and you become the words in this book. You tell me which words to write, and I am your poetry.

If I write from now on, all the time, from morning through night, then perhaps from now on you never will have left, and I will never have begun writing you, and love would be spelled another way.

For now.

Love, Sil

November 4, 2000
Dear Mil,

It's Sunday morning and I'm going through your letters again, my letters, more letters than I ever thought there were. I wanted to tell you, this is so strange to be editing my letters to you, as if you've died. And now I know, I have died with you, even though I am here editing our letters, which we are still writing. This letter would not exist, some would say, because if we are dead, none of them could exist. I say, you have not died, you have not gone. Not yet. You, staying, is who I write to.

Forgive me for sending these to be read by another. I have a need to fold them into an envelope, drop them into a mailbox, listen to them take off, wonder of their journey. I want to think of you opening them, turning the pages, rereading, smiling, thinking of what to write back.

I'll be here. Write when you can.

Love, Sil

Saying good-bye can be accomplished in many different ways. I said good-bye to Judy by writing her daily letters after her death and reading one of them at her memorial service. In Ray Bradbury's *Dandelion Wine*, twelve-year-old Douglas Spaulding says good-bye to his great-grandmother by writing down his feelings of anger, confusion, and sadness over her death. He says:

"YOU CAN'T DEPEND ON PEOPLE BECAUSE . . .
. . . they go away.
. . . strangers die.
. . . people you know fairly well die.
. . . friends die.
. . . people murder people, like in books.
. . . your own folks can die.
SO IF TROLLEYS AND RUNABOUTS AND FRIENDS AND NEAR FRIENDS CAN GO AWAY FOR A WHILE OR GO AWAY FOREVER, OR RUST, OR FALL APART OR DIE, AND IF PEOPLE CAN BE MURDERED, AND IF SOMEONE LIKE GREAT-GRANDMA, WHO WAS GOING TO LIVE FOREVER, CAN DIE . . . IF ALL OF THIS IS TRUE . . . THEN . . . I, DOUGLAS SPAULDING, SOME DAY . . . MUST. . . ."

When someone dies or moves far away and out of our lives, or turns their back on us and dies in a figurative sense, we need to express our sadness, loneliness, confusion, anger, and disbelief. We need to sort through these feelings, to let them out, to give them their own voice. One of the most beautiful examples of writing used to work through the loss of a loved one was created by C.S. Lewis. During the several months after his wife's death,

Lewis wrote his thoughts and feelings in empty journals he found lying about his home. His daily notes to himself in his extended journal, *A Grief Observed*, chronicle his day-by-day experience with the agony of bereavement and, eventually, his progression back to faith and to a sense of resolution. The following is an excerpt as Lewis nears the end of his final journal.

"In so far as this record was a defense against total collapse, a safety valve, it has done some good. The other end I had in view turns out to have been based on a misunderstanding. I thought I could describe a state; make a map of sorrow. Sorrow, however, turns out to be not a state but a process. It needs not a map but a history, and if I don't stop writing that history at some quite arbitrary point, there's no reason why I should ever stop. There is something new to be chronicled every day. Grief is like a long valley, a winding valley where any bend may reveal a totally new landscape."

Writing is a process of giving solid form to thoughts. As in C.S. Lewis's case, you can write every day for a period of time after a dear one passes away to work through the grief, loneliness, and confusion that accompany death. Through writing and looking back at your letters over time, you can observe the shift and change in your focus from extreme pain and loneliness to feelings that become, as a friend once described them, no less deep but very gradually not as huge.

Writing letters to a deceased friend or relative keeps the connection and the memory alive. When we write letters to those with whom we can no longer talk face-to-face, the person is there with us, watching over our shoulders, sitting across the table from us, listening, responding, sighing with delight over the attention we pay them. The strong sense of presence as we communicate in this way is not so different than when writing a letter to someone across the country. As we put down our thoughts, we feel an immediate connection with the person to whom we write. We know the letter will ultimately reach our friend, but the flow of feeling and emotion already moves in his or her direction as we write. Whether our letters are meant to be sent or to be saved, we write them because we have something to say and also because we enjoy spending quiet moments in thought of a friend.

By writing a letter on each birthday of a deceased friend or relative, you can honor the special person and also create your own written history of a loved one. Anniversaries, holidays, and the dates of special trips or celebrations that you enjoyed together are especially difficult times. By writing a letter, you acknowledge your memory of these precious moments and assuage the melancholy that emerges during certain seasons or on special dates throughout the year.

Another whole set of intense emotions arises when death happens before we are able to make amends, heal old wounds, and clear up misunderstandings. It feels unfair to be left with no way of saying such things as "I'm sorry" or "I didn't mean what I said" or "Why did you neglect me or do that to me?" By writing letters we are able to move these messages from our hearts, through our pens, and onto paper. We are able to spend time, spirit to spirit, with a deceased loved one, sorting out complicated, unfinished business. Although the strongest instinct may be to walk away from hurts that remain after the death of a loved one, facing the hurt holds promise of healing.

Think for a moment about how we learn to relax muscles by first tightening them. You can try and try to relax your hand by mentally concentrating on relaxing it, but what works better is to tighten your hand into a fist. Tighten, tighten, tighten the fist. Then, let go, and your hand relaxes more deeply than it would have by merely willing it to do so. In the same way, you can tighten and tighten your grip on the hurt that remains after a friend or relative dies by writing about the hurt from all angles, from inside out and upside down. And then you can let go and feel a release you could not have experienced without facing your emotion head-on.

Though such letters cannot be sent literally, they can be sent figuratively, and your spirit may feel all the better for having done so. What a beautiful ceremony it would be to write a letter filled with the emotions and memories that circle in your mind today about your deceased loved one, then wrap the message in a delicate envelope and send it skyward as ashes rising from the fireplace. Letters do not have to be carried by the United States Postal Service to reach their mark. They can be buried in the forest under the tree where you and your deceased friend once picnicked. They can be poems written on the first day of every month to your dear relative or friend and read aloud to the next full moon. When we need to reach out for healing and solace, there are effective ways to find comfort and release. Set aside the time, choose a meaningful setting, and fashion your message in a way that puts you in touch with the spirit of this special person in your life. Then, let your heart write the message that weeps inside of you.

Exercise: Begin the Good-Bye That Frees and Eases You

"My father's death had awakened in me an interest in the past. In Omaha we drove past the places I had lived in as a boy. The

houses seemed smaller, the hills and streets less steep, as if they had shrunk in my absence. . . . Never before had I set eyes on such a mockery of my remembrance."

—Wright Morris, *Time Pieces: Photographs, Writing, and Memory*

Some time after his father's death, Wright Morris traveled with his wife to visit his uncle's farm where he had once spent two weeks of a summer vacation. Later he wrote of the experience of reuniting with his aunt: "I can no longer distinguish between that actual meeting with Clara, in June, and the fiction I wrote about it that winter in California, the sentiments and nostalgia as palpable as the smell of pickling beets in the kitchen."

Experience becomes the story we wrap around it. Memory is like mercury between our fingers if not contained in a written capsule. Loss of a loved one pushes us into a corner where we want desperately either to relive, rewrite, or forever bury the story. Death makes us wish for something, anything else but an end to the story. Even if the memories are far less than good, the death of a loved one opens the pages of yesterday and recites the stories with the loudest voices.

At the death of a significant person, it is time to write. And to write the story of you and your special friend or relative, you need details. You need the smell of autumn red and gold burning in the bonfire you and your father made together each fall. You need the warmth of the flannel blanket being pulled up to your ears by your mother each night. You need the aroma of your aunt's Thanksgiving turkey roasting in the kitchen, or the fear and thrill of your cousin throwing you into the lake after he'd taught you how to swim. You need the comfort of your sister's hand rubbing liniment on your sunburned back, the sound of your favorite teacher reading "The Raven," the prickly excitement of your brother lifting you to place an angel on the Christmas tree. You need specifics that carry emotion on their wings, details that carry your relative back into the room, your friend back into your life for a moment.

Nudge 1

Now, bring the specifics to life in a letter. Picture the happiest moment you spent with a special person who is no longer with you, and write a letter describing it. If specifics do not come to you, pretend. The idea is to write a story in the form of a letter that will connect your spirit with that of your loved one.

Do you have a photograph of the two of you together that day? If you do, use it to carry you back into that moment. Use the photograph, or imagine you have one in front of you, to make believe. Pretend you are standing outside of the image and write as if you are the photographer who can see everything that is happening both inside and beyond the frame. Write about what happened before and after the picture was taken, how you felt when the exposure was made, what you and your friend or relative were laughing about, complaining about, dreaming about. In your letter, instead of telling your friend that she was important to you, paint a word picture of the closeness you shared in this photo-graphic moment.

Sample letter: from Bonnie Jean MacLeod, Cincinnati, Ohio. "This is just one of the many letters I have written to my sister since her death."
Good-bye moccasin woman,
    If you can read this, I love you. I love your old face and your

girlish voice. I love your stiff neck and your graceful hands. I love your bossiness, your tenderness, your shyness, your fierceness, your silences. Memories of you lie deep in my throat.

Of climbing trees, dangling our weightless feet yards above the ground. Leaves clapped softly as I looked up to you, one bough above. I climbed without you once, clung like a kitten for hours until your voice in my head said, "Just test with your toe until it's firm. Don't grab too close to the leaves."

We read Indian stories by flashlight, practiced Indian sign language in the basement, one of us holding the library book, the other dancing her hands. Our secret language. If only we could make up conversations about elks or moccasins at the bus stop.

Last year, your hair was long. A Cherokee maiden's braid down your back, woven to hide the bald patches. I combed it across your pillow. It was satin under my hands. After the funeral, Mother wrapped your TV in a white blanket and shoved it in my car. In the folds of the blanket was a long black hair. "The Indians believe every life is a circle." I read that a month ago, and I almost called you. "Whether we live seven days or seventy-seven years, we will accomplish all we were ever meant to do." We are all circles of different sizes, like the growth rings of a tree.

Now that you don't have to fight your sickly body you can climb oak mountains, swing from leaf tips. Now you are no longer my sister. Now you are Climbing Elk, the Quiet Moccasin Woman.

Sometimes the wind will blow a summer tree, making it swirl and shimmer as if there is a delightful child playing deep in the branches, but I know it's really you.

Nudge 2

Choose one specific trait about your friend or relative and write a letter by focusing on it. Pretend you are drawing a caricature of your loved one. Look for that one characteristic, talent, trait, gesture, act of kindness, quirk, accomplishment, or dream that you will never, ever forget, and write a letter about it. You might write about your dear one's taking up the violin at age fifty and becoming an accomplished musician. You may write about your grandmother's gorgeous shock of red hair that she collected from her brush in a porcelain hair safe on her dresser. You may write about your uncle's wild and wonderful storytelling that entertained family and friends at holiday gatherings, your father's picture-perfect golf swing, or your mother's baking every dawn to the delight of everyone who knew her.

SAMPLE LETTER: FROM ELIZABETH BRYAN,
W. ST. PAUL, MINNESOTA.

Dear David,

Someone asked if I ever felt your presence lingering somewhere in the air. I said I didn't. I said I wished I did. When you spoke you waved your hands up and down and sideways in the air, slender fingers fluttering fast as hummingbirds, silent as snow.

"David, did anyone ever tell you that you have gorgeous hands?" people asked you.

"Sure," you said and grinned at all of them.

At movies, concerts, anywhere we sat together, shoulders touching in the darkness, you and I always laced our hands. Like childrens' braids. And at this first concert without you, I sat beside Lydia and Max, clapped with all the others when

Jeffrey Tate, the Sommerfest conductor, hobbled carefully toward the podium, shoulders humped and twisted, beaming as he placed his cane beside his high stool, beaming at his musicians the way you always beamed.

Violists, cellists, violinists beamed back, raised bows.

In one long downsweep Jeffrey Tate's hands moved horns and strings and reeds in one long chord and lifting melody, hands in silent squares and rectangles and triangles, and I saw your hands, loose and graceful and narrow-fingered.

I saw you in the bookstore, hands arching in the air with stories of the sea, of sailing ships and captains and hurricanes. And I tried not to let my thoughts return to Dr. Lily Collins in that empty room two months ago, Lily's hands in mine.

"David's lungs are filling," Lily told me softly. "His X rays showed he isn't going to make it, Liz, not this time."

I watched Lily's eyes. She watched mine. What else was there to say, and Lily waited for me to understand, and we held hands. And then we cried, and Lily faced me, and we sat together until I let go of Lily's hands. Lily needed to go home and tend her children, and I had to dial telephones and tend to mine.

Jeffrey Tate's hands flew up and down in squares and circles, round and round, and you didn't have to be a widow to weep at Elgar's *Serenade*.

What made my fingers fly this morning through dresser drawers in sudden bursting busyness, fingers sorting, tossing, keeping? What made me open your nightstand drawer and pull out that envelope of photos? More family snapshots? Vacation scenes? Holidays with grandchildren?

I opened up the flap. Spread wide across a white sheet, nails shining and freshly manicured, your hands rested. Your hands.

Maybe, we thought six or seven years ago when you weren't able to find work, maybe you could model hands. And you made appointments, first-ever manicure and color photos for thirty dollars. All this for an agency who never called and, over weeks and months and years, we forgot about those pictures stashed in your drawer, you much too busy anyway describing books to customers at Hungry Mind.

What made me open up that drawer this morning to your hands, fingers long and slender spread wide across a pure white sheet like a blessing?

Nudge 3

Now that you have spent time dwelling on the happiness you shared with your loved one, you will begin to say good-bye by writing, "When you left, the . . ." at the top of the page. Finish this sentence twenty-five to fifty times, as quickly as you can. Then, choose one of these sentences as the beginning of a letter. Write for twenty minutes without stopping as you focus on this one response to "When you left, the. . . ." The next day write another letter, focusing on another of your responses. Continue writing from this list until you know in your heart that it is time to move to the next nudge.

Nudge 4

In almost all of the letters I have read that were written to deceased loved ones, the message of good-bye is actually a way of saying, "You remain with me still, but we are together in a new way now." Today you will write a letter to someone who is no longer with you, telling this person precisely how he or she remains in your life. When does this person appear to you? What causes you to think of him or her? What time of day or year, what season, what aroma or sound? What event or song, what piece of clothing or type of fabric brings him or her to mind? Does folding laundry fresh from the dryer remind you of your loved one? Planting pansies in the spring? Passing a Dairy Queen on a Sunday afternoon; hearing a Frank Sinatra love song on the radio; sitting in the old family wingback chair; reading a worn classic; seeing the geese fly overhead in formation; or picking wild raspberries behind your cabin by the lake? What, where, when, and how does your loved one come back to you?

Take at least twenty minutes today to tell your loved one how it is that the two of you connect these days. Come back to this exercise and write, write, write until you feel as though you have arrived at a method of being with your loved one that soothes your soul and would make him or her smile wide with joy.

SAMPLE LETTER: FROM SUSAN REILLY, GEORGETOWN, MAINE.
Dear C,

Tomorrow is the Summer Solstice, the longest day of the year. In my eyes it is a short-lived victory. No sooner does the Solstice pass than we begin the gradual, almost imperceptible, withdrawal into darkness. Yes, the roses will continue to bloom, the tomatoes will ripen, but "The force that through the green fuse drives the flower" will have begun its return to the roots where it will rest until the lengthening days come round once again. This year I think I will welcome that retreat. It is time to let this grief that has kept me at odds with the growing energy of spring withdraw quietly into the marrow of my bones.

Your son Dario stopped by for what an Indian friend of mine would have called "a flying visit," a few hours between trains on his way to meet friends for vacation. We had a quiet lunch at the hotel in town. He is a very fine young man. We talked easily together, and I felt, if you had been at a nearby table eavesdropping, you would have been pleased at that. He wanted to know chronology, to put events of your life he had heard about on a time line, and I helped where I could. He is shy, your Dario. And I thought as I watched him what I often thought as I watched you. "Youth is dangerous to all but the young." For in his self-consciousness and self-absorption, he could not have imagined that the shape of his eyes and the timbre of his voice brought you before me, or that his grief is different from mine. I feel sad that he should experience such a grief so young. I am afraid he will anticipate all grief will be like this one, and so he may fear the pain. How could I convey to him that every grief, like every love, is unique?

I went with him to the train station to see him off. As we said our good-byes, I slipped into his hand an envelope with a stone you'd given me and a poem I wrote that you had liked. I thought you wouldn't mind.

Now I am sitting here on the sun porch watching this evening unfurl over the sights and sounds so familiar to me. It is the time of day when things seem to be their most insubstantial. Funny how we humans like to think we get woven into a place while, in fact, the birds and the beasts do that more easily. We think we are woven into one another's lives and, for a time here and there, between trains, we are. But, in the eyes of the Divine, I think it is only love that gives us substance. And when we have loved enough then suddenly we become visible to the Divine, and welcomed home. An old woman's thoughts on an evening growing old.

So, tell me my friend, what should I do with these foolish letters? I had thought to give them to Dario but I know now that would not be fitting. We are on different paths, he and I. I think tomorrow, at the end of that most protracted evening, I will take some dried flowers I have saved, and these sheets, and go out in the garden and burn them all, an offering to the light that has run its full course. After I turn the ashes back into the earth, with the smell of smoke still in my hair, I will come in and lay myself down to sleep in the strengthening dark that wisely disdains words in favor of stars.

As always,

A

Nudge 5

Create your own tradition of keeping the memory alive. Write to your friend on each of his or her birthdays, on New Year's Day or another special holiday, every time you fly or every time you visit the mountains or seashore. Tuck your letters to this person into a beautiful box or urn, and reread them now and then. Eventually you will have created physical proof of the growth and insight that have happened by facing death as a part of living rather than trying to ignore it away.

EXTENDED SAMPLE LETTER: FROM JAMES W. HARKIN, FAIRFAX, VIRGINIA.

Dear son-in-law;

That January morning was freezing cold, but life was

good—a loving wife, a happy seven-month-old baby boy, and a master's degree, earned in the evenings, just weeks away. The roads were plowed leaving large patches of bare pavement. You stopped at a minimall and dropped off your laundry. The shirts to be starched, the slacks and suits to be dry-cleaned.

The traffic flowed smoothly. The road was clear, but your car skidded on a patch of black ice. The left front tire hit the curb with such force that your car spun like a top across the median strip into the oncoming traffic.

I met your wife, my daughter, at the hospital. It was too late. You were already gone. Your seven-month-old son, the towhead you carried in your big hand as if he were a football, was too young to realize his loss. Oh, the living you have missed.

With much sadness,

Your father-in-law, winter 1994

Dear son-in-law;

As I pen this, he is at my desk writing. "It's a story," he says. His tongue jutting from the side of his mouth as he forms the long, squiggly lines that are his words. He calls me Bumpa. It is a very special name to me. He is a little bear cub who likes the rough and tumble when we wrestle on the floor.

While shopping with his mother, he stopped to admire the men's ties and shirts. He asked when he could start wearing them. When he got to the boy's section, he picked out a red tie and button-down shirt. You would approve.

One day he spotted your rowing machine in our basement. I have it now. He asked what it was. When I told him that it had been yours, he was determined to try it. Of course, he's too short for it now, but he is growing fast. He is a very fine boy, and will grow into the kind of man you would approve of.

With a heavy heart,
Your father-in-law, spring 1997

Dear son-in-law;

We hang out often, your son and I. We go to the park where he plays with other children and makes friends easily. He notices when their dads are with them, and he watches carefully, observing what dads do.

During playtime, he sometimes races his little cars and trucks so that they crash into each other. I wonder what he thinks when he does this? He's so serious. It saddens me when I think of the scene he is innocently reenacting.

His grandma bought a big plastic dollhouse with some furniture and a little plastic girl for our granddaughter to play with when she visits. When he saw it, he insisted that grandma buy the daddy and mommy because the house needed a family. He always plays the daddy.

He has your worn old fielder's glove. I replaced the broken leather laces. He told me that he asks you to help him when he goes after a particularly difficult ball. His Little League baseball team won the playoffs, and he was given the team sportsmanship award. Before his name was announced, other team parents turned to his mother and said, "Your son should get it." You would have been so proud.

This winter he will be in a basketball league. At tryouts,

he dribbled the length of the court to the basket and made three out of four shots. He knows that basketball was your favorite sport.

Being an easygoing boy, he sometimes puts up with too much from other boys. I've told him that it is all right to fight back when somebody is bullying him even though he may get into trouble. Bumpas can do that.

Your son is now a tall, blue-eyed seven-year-old. He's always hungry, and is much harder to lift and throw over my shoulders than he used to be.

He is a very good student, reading way beyond his grade. He has a subscription to the children's version of *Sports Illustrated* and is fast becoming a sports trivia expert.

He likes family hugs. We form a circle with our arms around one another while holding him up in the center. He warms our hearts with his happiness at being surrounded by those that love him.

I sometimes accompany your wife and son on their visits to see you. He helps her replace the flowers and cut the grass around your headstone. Once when she was having trouble pushing the metal legs of a flower stand into the hard ground, he asked, "Will that hurt Daddy?" How do you answer a question like that?

Sorrowfully,

Your father-in-law, fall 2000

CHAPTER SIX

Honoring Your Heroes

"Hither the heroes and nymphs resort,
To taste awhile the pleasures of a court;
In various talk th' instructive hours they past,
Who gave the ball, or paid the visit last;
One speaks the glory of the British Queen,
And one describes a charming Indian screen
A third interprets motions, looks and eyes;
At every word a reputation dies."
—Alexander Pope, *The Rape of the Lock*

Thinking about heroes brings to mind Alfred Stieglitz and his photographic study of clouds that he called "equivalents." These come to mind for two reasons. First, there was a time, during my graduate work in photography, when Stieglitz was my hero. I read every word of his that I could find. I studied his moody portraits of famous friends and artists and of his wife Georgia O'Keeffe. I collected books that he had written or that offered reprints of his images. I explored New York City of the early 1900s through his romantic studies of the city's immigrants, workers, and changing architecture. As I said, Stieglitz was my hero. I wanted to photograph like him and write like him, and open my own American Place gallery.

And then the man fell from the pedestal where I'd placed him. As I further explored his images and writing, and as my photographic eye matured, I realized that I did not take to either his thorny personality or his most publicly seen portraits of Georgia. Over time Stieglitz became more man than hero in my eyes. And as he did, he grew more complicated, more mysterious, more human, and much more interesting.

As for Stieglitz's "equivalents," the artist created hundreds of images of clouds in an attempt to have them become the equivalent of his thoughts, hopes, fears, dreams, and despair. He wanted viewers to look at his images but, rather than seeing clouds, he wanted them to hear a symphony or to feel an emotion that went beyond subject matter. In a way, I believe we do the same thing when we create heroes out of human beings. We look at a man, woman, or child and see an equivalent of what we want this person to be for us. We ask more than he or she can give. We see less of the person than we would if we accepted him or her as human.

We demand that our heroes be like painted clouds that never rain down on us nor block the sun from our summer afternoons. In contrast, our nonheroic friends shift from cirrus to nimbus in an instant and we accept their fickle nature as normal. We understand their shade, their rain, their quick change of temperament. We accept the many faces of our nonheroic friends because they are like us and, as such, are fascinating, mysterious, and ever changing.

Eventually we learn that our heroes are not perfect beings. We may have thought them beyond reproach or criticism when we were ten years old, or in my case when I was in graduate school. But we learn over time that the people we believe to be the smartest, the wisest, the strongest, the kindest are human beings who have chinks in their armor just like the rest of us. It is natural for a little boy to believe his father who teaches him how to shoot baskets is the best athlete in the world. It is natural for a fourth-grade girl to believe her teacher is a poet beyond compare or her mother is the most creative woman who ever existed. We make heroes of our spouses, our older siblings, our friends, relatives, teachers, and caregivers. We turn professional athletes, world leaders, intellects, artists, and actors into heroes.

Heroic individuals enter our lives and affect us in sometimes enormous, sometimes almost imperceptible, ways. They inspire us to be our best selves. They show us the way to move toward our private dreams. They open doors that we might not have been able to open on our own. They lead us out of dark places and into the light. They give us a hand when we feel as though we cannot go it alone. And then something changes. Our spouse falls from his or her pedestal by doing something terribly human. We find out that our parent has made mistakes, has regrets, or has fallen short of his or her dreams and of our expectations. Our heroic friend moves away and out of our lives. Our mentor becomes too busy to take part in our activities any longer. The talent, intellect, appearance, agility, personality, focus, and passion of our heroes shift and slide into something other than what we remember and once revered. In the process we are left trying to balance the memory of what our heroes used to be with a feeling of regret and sadness for the loss of their perfect presence.

Exercise: Catch Your Hero as He or She Falls Off the Pedestal

"The way I see it, if you want the rainbow, you gotta put up with the rain."
—Dolly Parton

We demand superhuman acts from our heroes. Fathers cannot miss baskets. Mothers cannot burn turkeys. Counselors cannot be three minutes late to appointments. Doctors cannot be puzzled as to a cure for our ailments. We hold firm and tight to what we believe to be heroic qualities and to what we demand of those people in our lives upon whom we have conferred the title of hero. And then we hit the wall because demanding heroism from anyone ultimately leads to disappointment. When this disappointment happens, the path to feeling better about our heroes is to pay homage to the good that they provided us and to be honest with ourselves about what was not so perfect in their lives, their actions, or their characters. Writing letters to these people puts us in touch with the human behind the mask of hero, and it helps us confront the ambivalence we feel about our hero's human imperfection.

Nudge 1

Heroes don't necessarily move mountains. Often the smallest gesture makes a huge difference. List everyone you can think of who had a hand in creating your current identity and influenced your attitudes, beliefs, skills, and achievements. Next to their names, describe in as few words as possible why each was a hero.

SAMPLE LETTER: BY MONA DAVIS, PASADENA, TEXAS.
Sis, I'm thinking back . . .
November 17, 1971

I went to sixth grade today and stood a little taller. For today I got something very special, my lifelong dream come true. Eleven years on this earth I have wished for one thing, and today that wish became reality. I now a have a beautiful baby sister.

December 1971

Projectile. That's all I can say. How can one tiny, little body possibly contain so much liquid and hurl it so far, for so long, in such a projectile manner. I thought she was dying.

June 1973

She has crammed not one, not two, but several peanuts up her nose! Is this normal? I think we got them all out with the tweezers. At the age of fourteen and having recently obtained ultimate wisdom, I can safely say there is something not quite right about my sister.

May 1980

At last, college, and I am out of here! Finally, some privacy. No more annoying, little pest lurking, hovering, touching my things or babbling to my boyfriends. This could rank as the happiest day of my life to date. So, why isn't it?

May 1990

Her graduation day! My sister, the projectile peanut girl, graduating. She's beautiful and petite. I always wanted to be petite. She has blonde hair and blue eyes. Who doesn't want to have blonde hair and blue eyes? Eighteen, and the world is her oyster.

November 1994

I am probably too old to have a baby, but the deed is

done. After being sawed in half and having my eight-pound bundle removed, I can recall seeing two faces, my mother's and my sister's. I cried. They cried. I hurt. They hurt, only I know I hurt worse! Bravely, she stayed on for a week. She slept in a hospital chair, ran my errands, prepared my meals, and endured my husband. What a wonderful sister. What a wonderful friend.

August 16, 1997

Her wedding day. Is she old enough to get married? Truly my sister is grown and has become such a lovely person. Thoughtful. Generous. And, like our mother and her mother before her, she has a kind heart. She has added so much to my life. I always wanted a sister. This is why.

And this is why you, my sister, are forever my hero.

Nudge 2

Today you will begin a letter to one of your heroes. Look at the list of the people you began in Nudge 1 (page 111) who came to your aid in rough times, who helped you grow, who changed the course of your life, or who offered you friendship when you needed it most. Think back to your childhood, and include the teachers, friends, and relatives to whom you could turn for a good time, a kind word, or an answer to a pressing question. Think about the sports figures, artists, or men, women, and children you read about. Who did you look up to? Who made you laugh or taught you that it is OK to cry? Who listened to you when you were lonely or scared? With whom could you be totally yourself? With whom could you take a chance? Who showed you what it means to be strong or what it means to trust yourself? Add these people to your list, then write a letter to one of them, telling that person just how he or she touched your life forever.

Dear Ms. Rezeveska,

This is a message in a bottle that I am casting out to the universe, a mention of you in my prayers of thanks. This is a letter to the extravagant, gypsy-style librarian who taught sixth-grade library skills at Navy Yard City Elementary School in 1978. You befriended me, the shy, introverted wallflower that I was. You were the first teacher to reach out and inspire me. You encouraged me to write, to be an achiever in whatever I set out to do. You, the lady with the long brown hair piled high in a bun, with those greenish gray eyes and outrageous clothes. I would joke with my peers later that somewhere out there was a couch without a dust-cover because you had made that garish material into a fashion statement. But what did I know? Your heart was kind.

I can hear the bangles jangling on your wrists. I remember how you played Cat Steven's greatest hits and Simon and Garfunkel while we studied our lessons. How you always hurried to move the needle so as to skip the song "I'm ready to love, ready to love, yeah," perhaps thinking it too much for our innocent, young minds. Or maybe it was just an irritating tune to your ears. I never asked why. I merely took notice, as I did all your peculiarities.

You told me that you had read my school records, and I felt so flattered that someone cared enough to take an interest in me. You stopped to talk to me when you saw me in the halls. You comforted me the day I cried because my asthma kept me from running the timed mile with the rest of my classmates. You told me you couldn't run that mile either and gave me a hug. Such a precious and rare commodity in my world those days—your gentle encouragement. How you inspired me!

I remember the day you scolded me for misfiling a book on the library shelf. "Somebody doesn't know their ABCs," you snapped. "What is the matter with you people? You should know them backwards and forwards by now." How sharp the sting when such words came from the lips of someone I so admired. It was a little incident, but I was just twelve and, in my eyes, you were the greatest thing ever. I resolved to not let you down again. If you were good enough to believe in me, it was the least I could do to make an effort to get things right. So conditioned was I that your gift of friendship would be given or withheld based on my achievements or lack of them.

I remember trying out for a small role in the school play, and my delight when you asked if I would try out for the lead. Because of you I tried out and earned the role of Willy Wonka, in *Charlie and the Chocolate Factory*. We knocked them dead with each performance, and the knickname "Willy" stuck with me the rest of the year.

Your believing in me was a brew with powerful potency. No longer did I feel alone in this world. Someone was cheering for me in the wings. Your belief in my abilities saw me through high school where, you will be pleased to know, I graduated in the top 10 percent of my class.

There ought to be more teachers like you, who pause

and take interest, who stop to say hello, who encourage and inspire. It's been many years since high school and, though I still write nearly every day, my spelling is not all that it could be and my grammar slips in and out of proper form. But what needs to be said finds its way from my heart. You have probably retired, but I felt the urge to thank you for all you did for me. And for what it's worth, "Z, Y, X, W. . . ." Yes, I know them all backwards now, by heart.

Yours most sincerely, Willy.

Nudge 3

Write, "Just like you, I . . ." at the top of the page. Choose one of the people you listed in Nudges 1 and 2 (pages 110 and 112), then finish the sentence twenty-five times as quickly as you can. You may be surprised at some of your responses.

Choose one of your responses and write a letter to the person about your response—about how something in you reflects something in him or her. Explain how you feel about this similarity. Use other responses to elaborate, if you wish. Allow yourself to use this letter to dig deeper than you have gone before into what this person meant to you and how he or she affected your life.

SAMPLE LETTER: FROM LORI ZAYON DE MILTO, SICKLERVILLE, NEW JERSEY.

Dear Mom,

Half of my lifetime has passed since you left me, and the scab that grew over my heart has remained a steadfast companion these nineteen years. You were far too young to die, I far too young to cope. But somebody had to provide a center for the family, and it fell to me, as the oldest. I became a substitute mother, admittedly a poor one, to Marci and Lisa, and housekeeper and cook for them and Daddy. The carefree teenager vanished forever, replaced by a somber woman.

For years, I couldn't bear to talk about you. But I thought about you plenty, dissolving into tears at the slightest provocation: the sight of a tall, black-haired woman, the word "cancer" used in any context, movies in which anyone died of anything, a simple question about my mother, and most of all, Mother's Day.

Years passed, some good and some bad. Marci and Lisa grew up. Daddy learned how to be alone, because the women who offered him companionship simply weren't you. Absorbed as I was in my own loss, I never thought much about his suffering. Then I met and married Joe, in the same year that Lisa and Danny were wed, and I began to understand how potent love between a man and a woman can be. I'd remember how you two, married more than two decades, still held hands when we went out, and the glances that passed between you.

I felt guilty that I was so well loved when Daddy was so bereft, and compensated in the only way I knew how, by sharing my time with him. Today, we are great friends. I often wonder what you and I would have shared.

Your namesake, Lisa's son Zachary, is now two and a half years old. He has the face of the angel, enveloped in golden curls, but the rest of him is all boy. Lisa is as good a mother as I remember you being, eternally patient and loving, and Daddy a doting if not always helpful Pop-Pop.

When Lisa was carrying Zachary she went downstairs and saw you. She almost didn't tell me about it for fear I'd think she was crazy. Instead, I enveloped her in my arms, wiped away her tears, and honestly told her that I believed her.

It's comforting to imagine that you watch over us, Mom, and can see what we have become. We have learned to take all that life offers, because we know that it can end at any time. The tears which often accompany my thoughts of you are no longer harsh eruptions of grief and anger, but gentle tears of remembrance. I know now that you will always be a part of me, and that I will never get over missing you. I wish you a very Happy Mother's Day.

Love forever,

Your oldest daughter, Lori

Nudge 4

Write "I felt hurt when I learned that you . . ." or "I never thought I'd see the day when you . . ." or "You broke my heart when you . . ." at the top of the page. Finish the sentence, thinking about one or more of the heroes you listed previously. Use your own beginning sentence if one fits your situation better than those offered earlier. Then, write a letter with one of your sentences as a jumping-off place. Write for twenty minutes, letting your thoughts flow onto the page. Throw your lead sentence into the stream like a flower petal, and watch where the current carries it.

SAMPLE LETTER: FROM PAT WILLIAMS, HOUSTON, TEXAS.

Dear Dad,

We never discussed your approaching death. We simply

sat in your music room together, listening to melodies we had shared all of my life and the last thirty-six years of yours. That spring afternoon the piano strings of "Rhapsody in Blue," our favorite, communicated an unspoken tenderness we felt for one another. Our eyes spoke as we heard the majesty and beauty of song, lifting us together to another time when we both believed in your invincibility. As a young girl, I heard the rhapsody for the first time through your eyes and ears until the joy of the rhythmic sounds became my own.

At twelve, I learned to play, my fingers moving across piano keys on the old wooden upright. I practiced for days until I memorized your favorite song, "Deep Purple." The afternoon I played it for you, you cried. I understood that you knew how much I loved you. When I was a child, you fought a private war against alcoholism, a secret you kept from me. But somewhere along the time line of your life, a transformation occurred. Dad, we shared a deeper friendship then than I have ever known. Our song just like our love played on year after year, through my college graduation, marriage, the birth of my daughter, the labored times in my career, and my own personal war against alcoholism. The refrains were different, but the chorus always the same. "I love you" and "I love you, too."

Sometimes, when in the quiet of night I stare in the dark, the space you left is filled with song. Always, Your daughter

"When the deep purple falls over sleepy garden walls,
And the stars begin to flicker in the sky,
You wander back to me in the mist of a memory,
Breathing my name with a sigh."

Nudge 5

Now write a letter to another of your heroes. Pretend you are creating a documentary video of this individual. Relive one full, panoramic day during which your hero played an important part in your life. Bring the person and the situation to life by using all five senses in your description. Zoom in for a close-up. See the deep blue of your friend's eyes. Feel the touch of your hero's hand on your shoulder. Smell the fresh flowers your friend always kept on her kitchen table. Taste the tart lemonade your friend made for you each summer. Back up for a wide-angle view. Use this documentary approach to explain how your attitudes, philosophies, and relationships with others and yourself were formed, in part, by having known this person. Write for at least twenty minutes, and come back to this letter again if your first pass does not feel complete.

SAMPLE LETTER: JOANNE BERGBOM, GARDEN CITY PARK, NEW YORK.

Dear Myriam wherever you are,

I never told you about the day my mother screamed at me because I pulled the cord on the venetian blinds the wrong way, and she blamed it on you. You, my best friend, who were comfortably at home two blocks away. Not often given to such tirades, my mother surprised me with the vehemence of her anger toward you, anger unjustified in my mind. Forty years later I still wonder at her fear of our friendship nearly as much as I wonder why, at least once every summer when I sit down to write, your name comes unexpectedly through my pen.

You widened my world when you and your brother entered my sixth-grade classroom. You were the newcomer, older, more sophisticated, from Colombia. I probably would have offered friendship to any new student, but you provided me with a touch of the exotic as well. You caused me to make choices. It seemed natural that I chose you as a new friend, while my earlier friendships weakened and slipped away. We became "best friends" in a way I had not known before. Even though Roberta and I had vowed undying friendship, calling each other "the glue sisters" because we often refused to unclasp our hands, in truth, we were only playmates. With you I had a real best friend.

How delightful to discover you lived just down the block from me on Evergreen Avenue. As we shared confidences, I learned that our lives had more differences than similarities. You came to New Hyde Park from Ninety-second Street where girls your age—you were thirteen to my eleven—had serious boyfriends. You were a child of divorce and had been sent to America to boarding school, leaving your mother and two brothers behind. Your father had a second wife, and you lived with her and their children. In my two-original-parent world, I didn't know anyone else like you. Your father and stepmother spoke English with very heavy accents, and you called your stepmother Elizabeth. I think my mother was bewildered by all of this, but after exhibiting reserved disapproval, she let the friendship develop. She welcomed you into our home and usually let me spend long Saturdays at yours where we played canasta for coffee beans or built architectural masterpieces from an early version of Legos, or swam in your above-ground pool. I was with you when a new stepsister was born, and you were with me when my father died. Did the venetian blind episode occur before or after that? I don't remember.

My mother ranted about how my mind was always somewhere else—usually on you and what we might plan together. She raved about how I acted absentmindedly when I turned the blinds wrong way out. What she really was reacting to was my separating from family, becoming an adolescent, and stretching toward independence. She needed to blame someone for the fact that children grow up and leave home, and she chose to blame you. If she had had her choice, the blinds would have remained closed a lot longer.

For me, you were those growing years when the world was full of possibility, when I could tilt the venetian blinds in absentminded abandon, when the world came down to meeting under the corner street lamp and telling my best friend everything. I thought you'd want to know, wherever you are.

Best Friends Forever, Joannie

Nudge 6

"Writing stories has given me the power to change things I could not change as a child. I can make boys into doctors. I can make fathers stop drinking. I can make mothers stay."
—Cynthia Rylant, author of children's books

Give yourself time to digest what you have written to your hero. Allow yourself to reflect on the positive influences. Then, begin a letter in which you confront your hero, asking why he or she had to go away or why your hero did something less than heroic.

Tell the person how this other behavior affected you. Describe how angry, confused, lonely, and disappointed you felt when you realized your hero was not the best, smartest, wisest, or most talented person in the world.

Be honest with these feelings. Be direct. Let your sadness, anger, disappointment, or feeling of abandonment pour onto the page. This is your opportunity to set the record straight. This is your chance to loosen your grip on old feelings and to see your hero for what he or she is—human.

As you write remember that you can recognize the weak spots in the people you love as being human and, yet, not embrace these traits. Remember that you do not have to accept the hurtful or disappointing actions of your hero. You do not have to pardon the destructive things that he or she did to you or others. But facing and admitting the wrong done will allow you to shed some of the weighty sadness in your heart and to stop pretending the hurtful event did not occur.

When you are finished with this letter, read it aloud to yourself to see whether any speed bumps exist in what you have said or in how you have expressed it. You will know a speed bump when you come across one in your writing, because you will feel the same sort of tug in your chest that you experience when driving too fast over a rise in the road. You cannot read a less-than-honest sentence you have written without feeling a physical response. When you read your words aloud, you will realize if you need to rewrite a sentence, paragraph, or the whole letter to arrive at a more honest statement about how you feel toward your hero and what he or she has done to disappoint you. You may find that you need to come back to this letter several times, or write additional letters to this hero to get everything you want to say on paper—

or to get your message right with your heart. Once you are satisfied that you have been totally honest with your feelings and have expressed them in a way that feels true to you, move on to the final letter you will write to this hero.

Nudge 7

Finally, write a letter to your hero, explaining how good it feels to face him or her as one human to another. Describe how good it feels to be honest with your feelings, both positive and negative. Explore your new view of this person now that he or she is off the pedestal. Tell how you would like this person to act from this day forth. What do you expect of this person in your relationship, and what do you expect of yourself? If your hero wronged you badly, can you forgive him or her? Can you ask something of your hero that you never were able to ask before? Can you thank your hero for the positive influences upon your life while you forgive the negative? Or, has your opinion of what you once thought of as negative influences shifted a bit? Has your view of your hero's actions changed since you began writing these letters? If so, how? And what does this mean to your relationship and to your feelings about it?

Later, return to this chapter, and write an unsent letter to another of your heroes.

CHAPTER SEVEN

Clearing Up Monster Misunderstandings

"It is a capital mistake to theorize before one has data. Insensibly one begins to twist facts to suit theories, instead of theories to suit facts."

—Sherlock Holmes, in Sir Arthur Conan Doyle's "A Scandal in Bohemia"

Spoken communication is difficult. When we talk to one another, it is as though we play the childhood game of telephone, our story coming back to us with its words and meaning altered, added to, flipped upside down. Sometimes I feel as though my hearing is off with the number of times I realize that what I believe someone said to me and what they later tell me they said have no relationship to one another. At other times I'm certain I suffer from aphasia, because what I say and what others take my words to mean are as far apart as the Atlantic and Pacific Oceans.

I marvel that we can ever learn to converse in a foreign language since we rarely seem to understand one another while speaking in our native tongue. When we talk to one another, I assume we want to be understood, but we confuse the issue by employing nuance, slang, metaphor, regionalisms, and colloquialisms. Doing so makes language rich and fascinating, but it also bungles comprehension. In his syndicated column "The Writer's Art," James J. Kilpatrick offers the following sentence as a prime example of regional expressions that complicate our understanding one another. "He was poundin' on the table with his knife, just a-fawnchin' and a-slaverin' for his victuals." Interesting as such regional expressions are, try to imagine carrying on a conversation with many of these peppering the discussion. Consider how difficult it is to understand one another when, overnight, we begin talking about our favorite dessert as fro-yo, or discussing—IMHO—the success of a globoboss. New expressions like these are coined daily via the news, Internet, advertising, and entertainment and get in the way of our comprehending the millions of messages that constantly bombard us.

And if these language stumbling blocks were not enough, consider the havoc created by generation gaps, cultural vernacular, legalese, medicalese, officialese, and shoptalk. Think about the last time you visited your doctor and went away trying to figure out just what he or she told you about your health. What name was given to your problem? Why did it arise, what are you supposed to do about it, and what are the implications of treatment? Did you understand any of the description and instructions with both your stress level and the medicalese getting in the way of comprehension? And what about trying to understand what the auto mechanic has to say about the noise your car is making? The world is full of specialists all speaking their own private languages. We turn to them for assistance and feel confounded by the gobbledygook they feed back to us.

Even when we use easily understood words, their meaning in combination is often cloudy. Consider the seemingly simple question, "Want to do dinner?" When someone says this to you, is your friend asking whether you want to make dinner together, dine out together with your friend picking up the tab, or dine out together going Dutch treat? Is the person who puts forward the question asking for a date and, if so, what does that imply? These four little words, though seemingly basic and simple to understand, can be interpreted many different ways.

Communicating is just plain complicated when you consider the tricks of language that get in the way. When you add the fact that we approach one another from unique viewpoints and histories that match no one else's on earth, you begin to see why we so often misunderstand one another. Throw a little body language into the pot. Or, throw in the communication problems that arise when men and women try to discuss an issue, approaching it from unique and often divergent ways of looking at and dealing with the world. Then, think about communicating by telephone, so that facial expressions and body language are subtracted from what we usually use to understand what is being said, and the communication soup thickens.

My point in bringing up various pitfalls that influence how we transmit and receive information is merely to emphasize how sticky communication can be. We talk. We listen. Sometimes we understand; sometimes we don't. Sometimes we are understood; sometimes we're not. Sometimes we are good listeners; sometimes we are distracted and do not listen at all. Sometimes we connect; sometimes our words cause a rift. It is no wonder there are days when we feel an overwhelming desire to set it straight with someone, to unravel the confusion that sprouted out of a misunderstanding and remains like a pebble in a sneaker. And there is no better way to begin that process than by addressing your frustration in a letter that is for your eyes only.

SAMPLE LETTER: FROM BRIAN K. YAW, LA JOLLA, CALIFORNIA. "THIS LETTER, WHICH WENT THROUGH MANY DRAFTS BEFORE BEING SENT, PROVED TO BE A GOOD BEGINNING FOR A BETTER RELATIONSHIP WITH MY MOTHER," SAID BRIAN.

December 28, 1995

Dear Mom,

After talking with you on Christmas day, I felt saddened by your coldness. When I heard your message on my machine earlier that morning, it sounded as if you were angry. Today I received your Christmas card with your words, "Maybe someday you would like to be with us at Christmas again." My response is that I could say the same thing.

This is my seventh winter in California, and I feel at home here, in a place that is not only beautiful, but accepting. This is something I never felt in Nebraska. Growing up gay there was more difficult than you can imagine. Any love I felt, except from Grandma Arlene, was contingent on my being straight. Or at least that's how I felt. I now have friends who accept me unconditionally as a person. I have never felt the same from you. I wish I did.

Four years ago, after twenty-seven years of hiding and hating myself, I found the power within to accept myself as a person. Since then I have found people with whom I share unconditional acceptance. I surround myself with this type of nurturing as a substitute for what I don't feel from you. I am very lucky to have friends like Michael and Cathy.

When I told you I was gay, I was glad you didn't ostracize me; however, the silent nonacceptance is almost worse. Since I came out, I have had no visits from my immediate family. I have made two journeys home, only to find that although you want to see me, you don't want to "talk about it," as if "it" is a disease. Grandma Arlene accepts me as a gay man, and I love her dearly for it. I wish you could do the same.

I need to know that you care about me and my happiness, if we are going to have a real relationship. I had Christmas dinner at Mary's house this year. As you know, her two oldest children are gay. Two of Mary's best friends are a lesbian couple in their sixties. I was fascinated that she could be so understanding about them, as well as about her own gay children. And I felt jealous.

Mary made me think when she asked me if it was hard for you that I didn't come home for the holidays. When I told her that you have the other kids there, she said that she knew your whole life had revolved around us kids and that you missed me. I would like to believe this, but I can't help wondering if you only miss the old, straight, unhappy me.

I will not be an embarrassment to you or any of our family. I am comfortable and happy with my extended family of friends. But I am reaching out to you, Mom, to ask if you can and want to be a part of that family.

I love you, Brian

In your unsent letters, your written words remain as you arrange them. No one can disassemble, attack, or question them. No one can misconstrue them. No one can tell you that you should not feel as you do. You can write your heart out in your own, quiet place, then closely examine the words you choose to describe the misunderstanding that concerns you. On your own time, in your own uninterrupted fashion, you can use letter writing to clarify your feelings about a misunderstanding before you present your concern to someone else. This is your opportunity to see whether the misunderstanding grew out of a problem with word choice, difference in belief systems or viewpoints, or struggle for control. Perhaps the misunderstanding occurred because of poor listening, criticism, disinterest, stubbornness, blaming, or lack of maturity. Writing to yourself will give you the opportunity to dig down to the roots of the misunderstanding, to see it for what it is, and to find a way of growing through it into awareness.

Eventually, you may wish to write and deliver a letter to the person on the other end of the misunderstanding. There is no guarantee, however, that your friend or relative will want to either deal with your concern or work through the misunderstanding as you have done. I mention this because it can be a great disappointment to gain new understanding and, then, to learn that your friend or relative is neither interested nor capable of doing the same.

Growth is a personal endeavor and, much as you might like others to grow with you, if they make the choice not to do so, you must accept it. You cannot expect nor force others to see as you do, but you can work on your own spirit so it is as flexible, healthy, and peaceful as possible. Although it would be marvelous to have both parties erasing old misunderstandings together, it is more reasonable to explore the problem yourself, to share new insights with your friend or relative, and then to let go. As Anaïs Nin once said, "We don't see things as they are, we see things as we are." So, take responsibility for your own feelings and allow your friend or relative to do the same.

Exercise: Open the Door, Expecting Light on the Other Side

"All that we see or seem, is but a dream within a dream."
   —Edgar Alan Poe

Most of the time, misunderstandings are quite innocuous. For instance, on a day not long ago when my husband and I were driving home from northern Arizona, we stopped in a fast-food restaurant for a biscuit—one of my weaknesses when on the road. I placed the order. "Two biscuits, one plain and one with sausage, one small orange juice, and a small black coffee." The woman behind the counter repeated, "Two sausage biscuits, two coffees to go." I said to her, "Excuse me, but I ordered two biscuits, one with sausage, one plain, one small orange juice, a small black coffee." She called back to the kitchen, "One biscuit with egg, one sausage biscuit, small coffee with cream, one orange juice to go." We went back and forth like this while the line behind me grew longer and the rumbling of discontent grew louder. My husband and I poked one another like two eight-year-olds in a church pew struggling not to giggle at the sound of the soprano reaching for the high notes of "Amazing Grace." A curtain of confusion stretched between me and the person behind the counter. By some stroke of magic we finally were handed our order and left, thankful to be on our way.

I am not sure why the person behind the counter had such trouble understanding my words. Situations like this, which happen to all of us every day, magnify the fact that our reality and that of the people we come in contact with are usually worlds apart. If we can remember this and not take thoughtless actions that come our way personally, our days are less troubled. Being curious rather than furious about muddled communication allows us to see the humor in the moment and to stop anger before it drenches the day.

Nudge 1

You will now dive into an exercise about sorting through misunderstanding by using a bit of humor. To begin, make a list of ten recent times when you were misunderstood or when you misunderstood someone else. List both silly and serious incidents.

Choose the least serious situation and write a letter to the person on the other end of the misunderstanding about what happened. Write for twenty minutes. Don't stop or censor yourself. Let your words and sense of humor flow. Remember to be specific with your word choice. Tighter descriptions will take you closer to the core of understanding than nebulous, general terms. Thoroughly describe the colors, aromas, textures, time of day, month, and year. Describe your feelings, your impressions, your tone of voice, and your posture and gestures. Describe those of the person on the other end of the misunderstanding. Dissect the misunderstanding to get to the seed of it. Why and how did it take root? Did it ever get resolved? If so, how? Do you feel differently about the misunderstanding today than when it happened? If so, how? How do you think the person on the other end of the misunderstanding feels today? If you don't know, pretend that you do and describe that person's feelings.

Nudge 2

Next, choose the most serious situation in your list and write to yourself about it for twenty minutes, being just as free and open with your thoughts as you were with the insignificant situation. The misunderstanding may have happened yesterday or years ago. Whatever it is, dive into it. This is not the time to mince words or step lightly around the subject; this is the time to let it rip, feel the passion, and begin to work through the hurt caused by communication that didn't hit the mark with someone important in your life. Talk to yourself about the people involved in the misunderstanding, the events leading up to it, and the feelings that grew out of it. Clarify for yourself how the misunderstanding has affected your life, your attitudes, your ability to sleep and eat, and work and play. Discuss what you did to clear up the confusion and what the result of your efforts was. Talk about how you feel differently about the misunderstanding today than you did when it occurred. Write for twenty minutes.

Nudge 3

Now write an unsent letter to the person on the other end of this serious misunderstanding. Begin by explaining how you felt when the misunderstanding occurred. Be honest, but pretend that you are going to send this letter and watch to see how the tone differs from the letter you wrote to yourself. Remember, however, that this is your opportunity to get withheld feelings off your chest and onto paper. If you felt angrier than you have felt in a long time, say it. If there was another event that caused you to feel just as strongly, use it as an example to describe your reaction to being misunderstood. Turn to your thesaurus and dictionary to get clearer and more specific with your description. Instead of using broad statements such as, "I feel bad," get more to the point by saying such things as, "I feel lonely, abandoned, rejected, frustrated, or resentful." Instead of saying, "I feel hurt," tell exactly what you experienced, such as, "When you told me to leave and never come back, I ached as if I had food poisoning. All I could see in front of me was emptiness, and I felt sad, lost, and angry all at once."

You may need to write more than one letter before you are satisfied with the way you have described your perception of the misunderstanding. Be certain that your letters include discussion of what it is you intend to do to clear up the confusion and what you hope for in response from the person to whom you are writing.

Nudge 4

The next day, write another letter to the person on the other end of the misunderstanding. This time describe the response you would have enjoyed receiving instead of the one that he or she directed toward you. Once again be as specific as possible. A sample beginning of a letter: "Dear _____, It would have made a world of difference to our relationship if you would have asked me why I had to go away for a while rather than yelling that I am just another heartless guy who should immediately get out of your life forever."

Pretend you are talking face-to-face with the person on the other end of the misunderstanding and describe what might have happened had there been a little more compassion, patience, empathy, or even sense of humor between the two of you. Tell the person what you would like to do now about the misunderstanding and how you plan to prevent these events from occurring in the future.

Nudge 5

Now write to yourself, pretending you are a friend or relative who has been watching the serious misunderstanding unfold. It is common for us to talk about our everyday problems with someone whose opinion and response we value. Pretend that your confidant has been listening to you, watching the misunderstanding take its course, and now reveals his or her opinion about the situation. See what you can learn by allowing this person to write through you for twenty minutes. Allow the person to assess the misunderstanding from his or her point of view and to suggest what you could do to (1) get beyond your hurt feelings, and (2) prevent such misunderstandings from happening in the future.

Continue to write twenty minutes each day in your voice or in that of your confidant about this misunderstanding until you feel as though you have learned something new about how you can deal in a more effective, compassionate, open-minded fashion with the important people in your life. Write until you experience a positive shift in your feelings about a major misunderstanding. Write until you feel as though a door has opened and you have walked through it into greater understanding.

Nudge 6

Now that you have dealt with some specific misunderstandings in your life and have come to greater understanding about why they happen, write a letter to yourself, discussing the reasons why you are sometimes not understood and why you sometimes do not comprehend what someone else is saying. Refer to examples to clarify the various instances when misunderstandings take place. As you describe the common causes for confusion between you and the people in your life, explain how you intend to jump over or take a detour around these stumbling blocks when they occur. Begin your letter today and come back to it when additional causes for misunderstanding occur to you. Use this letter to continue improving the way you relate to others. It is easier to avoid trouble when you know what causes it and are aware that you can take measures to improve the way you communicate with those around you.

CHAPTER EIGHT

Granting and Asking for Forgiveness

"Forgiveness is the key to action and freedom."
   —Hannah Arendt

S ome years ago my husband and I decided to build a dream house on a piece of rolling desert spotted with saguaro and inhabited by coyote and javelina. We signed a contract with a builder, investigated countless architectural options, pored over hundreds of interior decorating and landscaping details, and paid each draw as it came due. The foundation was poured, and walls and a roof took shape, but then a crack appeared in the romance of the process. The builder fell short of holding up his half of the bargain. He did not oversee the work as paid to do. Then he refused, after the closing, to remedy major faults that were built into the house during his absence from the site. We were left with heaps of sadness, inconvenience, and repair bills in correcting the faulty construction.

I lived through the experience with feelings of hurt and anger. I would awaken in the morning with bitter dialogue roaring through my head like a freight train and fall asleep at night still talking in nails-down-the-chalkboard tones to myself about the situation. I wanted the builder to be honest. I wanted him to be responsible. I wanted life to be flawless. I was unrealistic. Life does not flow without bumping against boulders. People do not exist who have no faults and who do not, upon occasion, turn their backs upon responsibility. Intellectually I realized this, but my heart and soul fought hard against accepting reality.

Eventually, however, I grew tired of the builder's control over so many of my waking and sleeping moments. I needed to shed the cloak of anger I wore about the building experience, so I used a divert-your-attention technique to do so. Every time a thought about the builder came into my head, I yelped a loud, wild cry. Lucky for me these thoughts most frequently cropped up when I was alone; otherwise, the technique would have been frightfully embarrassing. It took only two or three weeks of shifting from the angry thoughts to wild banshee yipping before my anger stopped surfacing altogether. The magic technique helped me to gradually feel, on the surface, as though I had let go of the burden of resentment I'd carried for a long time.

It wasn't until recently, however, that I felt as though I'd finally forgiven the builder and had thoroughly disintegrated the thorny seed of anger that rested in the corner of my heart. Until recently, forgiveness of him was beyond my reach since I thought that accepting his wrongdoing was a necessary part of the process. With a little research and a lot of writing to myself, however, I came to understand and accept a different concept of forgiveness. I learned that the Greek word that is often translated as forgiveness was used in ancient times to indicate release from an office, marriage, obligation, debt, or punishment. It had always been obvious to me that something being owed was inherent in the concept of forgiveness. I'd just never thought of forgiveness as simply a voluntary nullification of a debt.

As long as I harbored the feeling that the builder owed me

something, I carried anger and resentment with me and remained stuck in the past with an old, worn-out hurt. What I needed to do was get the power back into my own hands. I needed to take equally good care of my emotional self as I do of my physical self by eating right, exercising, and taking my vitamins. Once I let go of the debt the builder owed me, I freed myself of the negative emotion tied to it and moved out from under the sadness I'd worn for too long.

Forgiveness of someone is just the other half of caring enough about your self to avoid continued injury and pain. In my case with the builder, until I realized that forgiving does not imply accepting the wrong done and does not necessitate condoning or giving an OK to it, I felt as though I could not forgive and walk away. Once I realized that forgiveness is merely canceling the debt, I was able to turn my back on the pain it had caused, gleeful that I'd made the decision not to live with the anger forever.

"A wise man will make haste to forgive, because he knows the true value of time, and will not suffer it to pass away in unnecessary pain."
—Samuel Johnson

SAMPLE LETTER: FROM ANGELA LAM, SANTA ROSA, CALIFORNIA, A WOMAN WHO NEEDS TO FORGIVE HERSELF.
Dear Ed,

I should have told you this long ago, but I'm writing a letter instead. The time is gone. The "not now, maybe later" has become the present and you are not here.

When I was washing dishes, years ago, you came up behind me, wrapped your arms around my waist, and nuzzled your big "French Tickler" nose against my neck. And I pushed you away to turn down the heat of the oven, to rescue the wilting spinach, to reprimand our son for climbing on the sofa once again. When you persisted in your advances, I said forcefully, "Not now, maybe later." You slinked away, forgotten and ignored, and I finished preparing the meal. We ate in an undercurrent of strained friendliness. Your feet kept rubbing my toes beneath the table even as I tried to shove mashed peas into our son's helpless mouth. Being a mother of a disabled son is difficult, I told you, but you already knew. You spent many evenings rocking him to sleep, many nights sleeping beside him, cradling his neck so he could breathe.

I wish I could hear you breathing now. I should have said, years ago, that I love you more than anything. Should have, but didn't. Now all I have to comfort me is the ghost of your arms around my waist. "Not now, maybe later." We only have now; there is no later.

Love, Your Sorrowful Wife

In his book *Forgive & Forget: Healing the Hurts We Don't Deserve*, Lewis B. Smedes says, "If we say that monsters [people who do terrible evil] are beyond forgiving, we give them a power they should never have . . . they are given the power to keep their evil alive in the hearts of those who suffered most. We give them power to condemn their victims to live forever with the hurting memory of their painful pasts. We give the monsters the last word." But we don't need to do this. We can use various techniques to turn our backs on the past and focus on the love, goodness, and people in our lives that help us to be our best.

The ancient notion of forgiveness as canceling the debt concentrates on the present, which we can control to some degree. What happened long ago or yesterday is out of reach, beyond our ability to change or erase, but the present is here for our molding and shaping. Choosing to be realistic about what we can control, choosing to be as healthy and peaceful as we can be rather than holding tight to vengeful, angry, and resentful feelings, is as much within our grasps as turning several ingredients into delectable bread for our dinner table. Just as we make bread because we love the process, the taste, and the nutritional benefits of the food, we forgive because we care about ourselves and want to be healthy and at peace. We feed and care for our spirits when we say, "Enough. I'm taking the power back. I'm canceling the debt, stilling the voices of yesterday, and choosing to think and act in ways that promote my well-being."

Now, the one example I have referred to from my own experience is insignificant when compared to the misery of war, murder, incest, and abuse. It may be insignificant when compared to the hurts you have faced. The weight of the situation, however, is not the point. Every day, life flows over us with joys that we can relish and with hurts that we are better off forgiving. Take, for instance, the man who steals your parking space, the friend who forgets the lunch date she had with you, the person you care for who harms you physically or emotionally. However great or small the wrong done to you, the process of moving beyond it is the same. Although it may take much longer to forgive the huge wrongs done to you than the insignificant ones, the first step in taking back your spirit remains the same—accepting the pain that a person or event brought into your life. You must realize the power the experience has held over your existence. Then you must work toward reclaiming control of your spirit, calling it back so it no longer rests in the hands of the person who wronged you but rather in your own care and tending.

Exercise: Take the Power of Your Life Back Into Your Own Hands

> *"Forgivers . . . are not content to be stuck in a quagmire. They reject the possibility that the rest of their lives will be determined by the unjust and injurious acts of another person."*
> —Beverly Flanigan, *Forgiving the Unforgivable: Overcoming the Bitter Legacy of Intimate Wounds*

As with the other exercises in this book, working toward the forgiveness of someone necessitates concentrating for a while on a painful experience. I would like to emphasize once again that spending time with the pain is merely a single step—but a very important one—in the process. Telling the story of the painful experience gives it solid shape and form. It begins to break down the mystery that shrouds the experience. Think of it like wiping the steam off of a windowpane to gain a better look at the nebulous shape lurking on the other side.

Rather than turning your back on a hurtful experience as if it never happened and meanwhile wondering why you live in a fog of unhappiness, discontent, and resentment, face your pain today. Prove that you are stronger than the memory, stronger than the person who hurt you. In her book *Anatomy of the Spirit*, Caroline Myss, Ph.D., says, "Forgiveness is a complex act of consciousness, one that liberates the psyche and soul from the need for personal vengeance and the perception of oneself as a victim. More than releasing from blame the people who caused our wounds, forgiveness means releasing the control that the perception of victimhood has over our psyches."

You begin to stop being the victim of memories when you live in this moment, choose to make a change in the way you feel about the past, and let go of debts connected to yesterday. You begin to take back the power you need to be at peace when you accept yourself as able and worthy of cutting the ties to a wrong that was done to you.

Nudge 1

"Forgiveness is the fragrance the violet sheds on the heel that has crushed it."
—Mark Twain

Begin a letter to yourself with the declaration, "I didn't deserve this experience, I didn't bring it upon myself, and I don't choose to continue living with the emotion surrounding it any longer." Continue with a description of one particular wrong that was done to you. Tell your story as if you are on a train in a foreign land and a kind stranger who you will never see again invites you to tell about your life. Feel totally at ease opening your heart and laying bare the story of your greatest hurt. Tell the stranger everything. Know that this person hears and understands but has no reason to judge or to repeat what you say. Hold back nothing as you relate your story.

This letter may take several writing sessions. It may take a month to complete. It will, no doubt, scratch old wounds and open old sores. But the process is necessary, for just as you cannot let go of a mist that wisps away as you try to grab it, you cannot let go of a nebulous hurt until you examine its parts and give it solid, written form. So imagine the stranger asking questions about your experience, and answer openly and honestly. Write until you feel as though the entire story of the hurtful experience is told. Write until you hear the stranger say, "I understand what you have told me. As I leave you, I carry part of your pain away from you. When thoughts of this experience surface again, write to me. Send your hurt to me in letters. I will be there for you, ready to listen and watch as you grow stronger than this memory."

Nudge 2

Now that you have immersed yourself in the story of your hurtful experience, you are ready to step back for a moment. Read your letter or letters aloud, taking note of the words and phrases you used to describe what happened to you. Read slowly. Pay attention. Are there words or sentences that you would change today? If so, put a line through these and write more suitable descriptions above them or in the margins of your letter. As you reread your letters, consider the following questions, then rewrite any letter that does not feel authentic.

- Did you use words of anger, resentment, criticism, and hostility? If so, would you change any of these words today, with either stronger or softer descriptions? If you make changes to your letter, explain why you are doing so. Were you softpedaling in your first letters? Were you hiding something? Were you afraid of being totally honest?
- Did you talk about wanting to get even? If so, do you feel the same today, or has this desire lessened or become even stronger?
- Did you talk about blame in your letter? If so, has your feeling changed about who is to blame for your hurt?

- Did you talk about life being unfair? If so, how do you think life should be different for you, and why? Do you think life owes you something? What does life need to be in order to be fair? Is there another way to think about life that will cause you less sadness and disappointment?
- Did you discuss the stress, depression, anxiety, or fear that you experience today because of this past event? Do you have anything to add about how the event continues to affect your life today? Did you talk about how this past event has affected your relationships with people, your job, your ability to play, your ability to create or to feel good about yourself?

As you read your letter(s) aloud, beware of sentences that make you pause or that make you feel as though you are skipping a beat. These reactions to your writing are sure signs that what you have written is off the mark. Use the previous questions to test your story for authenticity. It is our nature to exaggerate or downplay, to add or subtract color, to go too far or to stop short as we dig into what we remember of the past. As you tell and retell your story to the stranger on the train, you will know when you arrive at the truth. Your inner wisdom will tell you when your authentic voice is speaking. There is no right or wrong story that you can tell, but there will be stories that feel either off base or genuine.

When you are satisfied that you have told your tale in as honest, open, and thorough a fashion possible, make a date with yourself to come back to this exercise in one week, in one month, or in six months, to see how your story feels at that time. If your feelings about the event shift and change, or if your understanding of the event deepens, make note of this growth. Retell the tale or parts of it to reflect the changes in your attitude or feelings.

Nudge 3

Write a letter to yourself today, considering the possibility that the hurtful event didn't happen to you because you're *you*, but just happened. Consider the following in your letter:

- What is the possibility that the person on the other end of the hurt would have mistreated anyone in his or her reach? Not that this excuses the action and not that it lessens your pain, but considering the notion enables you to shed the feeling that the mistreatment was directed at you because of something you did or something you are.

- Have you harbored feelings that you were somehow to blame in the event? If so, what do you think you did, or what is it about you that brought on the hurtful experience? Are you being honest with yourself as you answer this question? Would your best friend agree with your answer?

- Do you feel as though life picked on you because this happened to you? If so, what do you believe about life that supports or negates this feeling? Does it serve you well to feel as you do about what you deserve in life or how life has treated you? Where did you learn this belief? Do the people most important to you believe the same?

- How would your feelings change if you were able to accept the fact that the hurtful person in the event was the problem and that you were not? Is it possible for you to accept this notion?

- If you feel as though you were part of the problem in the hurtful event, is there something about your actions, personality, habits, or relationships with people that you could change to prevent a similar event from happening again?

Begin today's letter: "When I walk around the backside of

this thing that happened to me, I can see that. . . ." As you write pretend that the listener on the train knows when you are telling the truth and will stop you when you are being insincere or covering up your real feelings. The object with this exercise is to free yourself of blame and to see that no matter how much you try to be in control, life events often rain down on you without your inviting or expecting them. It is not your fault that these events take place. It is not in your ability to stop the rain, nor does it fall because of something you did. Storms just happen. Your job is to gather the water for recycling, leave the scene, or open a huge umbrella. Writing letters to yourself about the storm will help you discover how to survive and grow stronger during such times.

Nudge 4

Now you are ready to write a letter to the person on the other end of your hurt. This letter will not be sent, so write honestly and openly. Hold nothing back about your feelings toward the person and the hurtful event. This is your opportunity to address the person involved in this difficult situation as you have always wanted but feared to do.

Too often we believe we somehow deserve what has happened to us, but our tendency to do so is a defense mechanism that allows us to keep from admitting hurtful truths to ourselves. No one deserves hurtful experiences; they just happen. Remember this as you write your letter today. Tell the person you address that you did not deserve his or her mistreatment. Tell the person how you felt when you were wronged. Explain how the event has affected your life, your self-image, your relationships with others, and your ability to do your work and to enjoy your free time.

Once again you may need to write more than one letter to cover all that you want to say. Take as much time as you need. Understanding comes with clarity, and clarity does not come quickly. It takes time, concentration, and patience. So give yourself the time you need to empty your heart of its memory of hurt, anger, and disappointment.

SAMPLE LETTER: FROM BARBARA GRYTE, SUNRISE BEACH, MISSOURI.

R . . . . .

The gaudy neon lights accompanied by the now familiar organ music soon give way to the screams and the deafening rumble of the car. It is a repetitive dream that invades my nights. Exhilaration and anticipation, the fear and regret, the loss of control and the wish to stop the ride and get off. The metaphor seems trite, a simple and sad summary of the many years we spent together.

You were, at first, so caring, giving, loving, respectful, and honest. I could never have foreseen our future. I know the history that set you on your path, the negative impact your mother had, the years of anger and bitterness, both of which were ferocious and frightening and erupted frequently, and mostly unjustifiably, during our marriage. Your angry explosions were answered by my tendency to absorb the guilt, a response you were quick to recognize and exploit. The more guilt I felt, the more determined I became to be the perfect wife, anticipating your every want and need, so you would love me. I rewarded your displeasure.

The monetary deprivation of your youth focused your professional energies on acquisitions—measuring your success in life in square feet and horsepower. Possessions, however, often sat forgotten and unused. The anticipated happiness in acquiring a possession never seemed to materialize. And anger often followed at the lack of time to enjoy such things because of the hours of work required to pay for and maintain those very possessions. It was a vicious cycle you never understood.

You prided yourself on your devotion to medicine, which you viewed as a calling. You were blessed with near genius intelligence, a gifted diagnostician; your patients were appreciative and in awe of your abilities. You gave them your time, your devotion, your emotion. Your family was the recipient of whatever was "left." We learned our place in your life. The children saw other physician fathers arrive at the tennis matches, the band concerts, the awards assemblies. They never understood. I made excuses for you, explained away your actions and words, smoothed the waters, tried to keep the semblance of a family unit. Despite your high intellect, you were dysfunctional when it came to relationships.

A deep-seated anger and insecurity festered in your psyche, controlling your misdirection. Infidelity became the coping mechanism for your unhappiness. The betrayals destroyed much of my spirit, and my ability to analyze and understand the reasons and the realities of your words and actions did nothing to ameliorate the emotional devastation that you created.

And then your health began to deteriorate. Multiple conditions worsened and left you in constant pain, eventually requiring daily morphine. You had to give up most of the interests and hobbies that you once loved. When most men would have given up and given in to their disability, you were determined to continue to be productive. I felt sorry for you, and I admired your grit. Over the years you had gradually alienated family, friends, and professional associates. You were alone, isolated, unhappy, unhealthy, and unable to understand how you got from point A to point B. I couldn't leave.

And then, you died. Your family sat dry-eyed at the funeral. Your patients wept. That was, after all, appropriate. The other day as I walked into the attic to retrieve a box of papers, I glanced in the dimly lit corner at a stack of dust-covered boxes —three boxes containing the material representation of your life. It should all come down to warm memories—a point you missed completely. And now for all of us, the memories are dimly lit and dusty as well.

The curious probably wonder at my short-lived mourning . . . the ring I removed after six months, the photographs missing from the bedroom, but I refuse to continue living the lie that was our marriage. I try not to dwell on wasted years and opportunities forever lost, and I pray that soon I will find forgiveness for us both. And, when I sleep, I pray the dreams will be no more. . . .

Barbara

Nudge 5

To this point you have looked at a hurtful experience, have addressed the person who mistreated you, and have moved from dwelling in yesterday to focusing on today. Now you can let go of the debt that still connects you to your hurt. You can forgive.

Write an unsent letter to the person who wronged you, explaining that although you do not condone his or her treatment, you no longer want to hold tight to the feeling that he or she owes you something or that you wish to get even. Explain that you no longer expect him or her to be perfect, loving, responsible, present, or understanding. You no longer expect anything but instead are turning your attention toward feeling positive about yourself and the world around you. Describe how you no longer want to view the world through glasses colored by anger and that only by breaking with the past will you be able to do this.

Nudge 6

Sometimes we need to forgive the wrongs done to us. Sometimes we need to seek forgiveness for a hurt we inflicted upon someone else. Today you will write a letter asking for forgiveness. Look into your heart for sadness that connects with an act that was less than kind. Write to the person whom you treated thoughtlessly, explaining the circumstances surrounding your action. Explain why you did what you did, how you felt afterward, and how you feel today about your actions. Apologize for your thoughtlessness, ask the person to understand and forgive you, and promise to be more loving in the future.

In the process of writing your letter, search for new awareness concerning the wrong you did. Do you understand your action better today then you did at the moment? What have you learned since your hurtful act about yourself and your place in the world that will keep you from repeating such an act? Before you leave this nudge, write a short note to yourself, forgiving yourself for committing a wrong. Add that you accept yourself as being human and therefore fallible. It is not necessary to like what you did or to condone it, but you can cancel the debt (and the feeling in your heart) that you must pay penance forever for your hurtful act. It is as important an act of kindness to forgive yourself as it is to forgive those who bring hurt into your life.

SAMPLE LETTER: FROM CAROL BINDEL, FOREST HILL, MARYLAND.

Dear Mother,

I want you to know that my divorce sickens my soul, too. Yes, I saw it in your eyes, that disappointment with hearing that one of your daughters planned to divorce.

Early on, when the troubles began in my marriage, I memorized I Corinthians 13 about how love is patient and kind, not jealous nor boastful, bears all things, believes all things, hopes all things, endures all things. I know it was by your example that I learned to love, and from your example that I knew of a place to search for an enduring definition of love. But I'm just not good enough to love like that.

This struggle pulls and twists me so. It reminds me of what happened when I came home from college that first time, with my hair cut off. You stood at the end of the walk, at the gate of the old metal fence, tears collecting in your storm-gray eyes and spilling down the creases of your face you always called your laugh lines.

You cried out, "Your beautiful hair! How could you? Your crowning glory! How could you desecrate yourself so, to cut your hair? Oh, daughter, how could you?"

I looked at you, not knowing what to say, and saw anew

your own hair, maybe a little whiter, but still parted in the center and swept softly up and back over your ears, wound into the coiled mound on your head. Your "topknot," so much hair, nearly covered the back of your head. Uncoiled at night it streamed down your back and onto your hips in a soft tumbling flow. Beautiful hair.

Your covering of white net, a cap fashioned with its wide smooth front yolk and pleated, shaped back, fit over your topknot. The Plain-people version of a prayer veil; your covering, like your uncut hair, serving as an outward sign of your inward choice of obedience and devotion to God.

There I came, your youngest daughter, with the short shag haircut popular in the sixties, a haircut shorter than an Amish boy's. I didn't need you to elucidate how you saw my short hair. I knew by your weeping at the gate. It was as if I were looking into a full-length mirror through your eyes. I'd gone modern, and you were betrayed. I was ashamed, seeing myself through your eyes. But bravado prevented my admitting it. That haircut was part of my bid to establish independence. You held out your arms and hugged me, anyway.

You enfolded me and touched my cheek with your tear-wet, laugh-lined cheek. Now my divorce betrays us both in ways deeper and more lasting than any hairstyle ever could. Is divorce the result of having gone modern? Will you still hold out your arms to me? I hope so because, in spite of it all, or more likely because of it all, I love you Mother. I still need you, depend on you for guidance, and trust you in ways I trust no other. Please, love me anyway,

Your daughter, Elizabeth Ann

AND ANOTHER, WRITTEN YEARS LATER. CAROL SAYS: "WITH THIS LETTER, I THINK I'VE TAKEN MY OWN LAST STEP IN UNDERSTANDING THE SOMETIMES TORTUROUS PATH MOTHER AND I TROD."

September 15, 1986

Dear Mother,

All those years of writing to you; never once an answer.

We found them in your dresser, tied with blue lace seam binding, all these letters I sent you over your years in "the home." Now I sit here with them lying on the table in front of me. They exude an odd scent, some mix of lavender and Murphy's oil soap, scents I always associated with home.

Here I am with all my letters. Accumulated for all those years. The logical part of me explained over and over in that time that you couldn't answer, having dementia, not even remembering me since the time of Papa's death. I didn't know, then, why I wrote. What was the use? What difference did a letter make now and then from a daughter already obliterated in the mists encroaching on your mind? Every logical part of me screamed, "Useless!" And yet, another part I couldn't identify then insisted I keep writing.

Did you tie up the first letter packets? Using lace seam binding is just the sort of thing you would have done, especially if you had a hank of it around. Did someone read the letters to you? Did you understand some of them? Sometimes?

I've read them all again; now I know why I wrote. The first years, I wrote with the hope that you would remember me occasionally, and understand me, at least in part, sometimes. I wanted you to forgive me for the differences we'd had. Then I started discovering myself in the process.

That discovered self, dearest Mother, is truly your daughter, more like you than I once would have dreamed possible. I've discovered how strong and good an example you set, and I'm proud to find ways I'm just like you. I believe you knew, or at least trusted, how your children would mature. How often I heard you read from scripture, "Train up a child in the way he should go, and when he is old he will not depart from it."

The training you gave me in my first twenty-four years has molded me in ways I'm still discovering a decade and a half later. Now I know that for as long as I live your voice will echo in my mind, and your forming influence on my life will carry through to my own death. You are an intimate, inseparable part of me. As mother and daughter, we are irrevocably linked, were so linked from the moment of my conception. Did you know that already then? At forty-five, your age at my birth, with all the life experience you had already earned, I'd guess you did. After all, you had a mother of your own, and daughters before me. You were older when I was conceived than I am now, and had already been holding up your chin for years. You knew about how it is with mothers and daughters.

You never answered even one of my letters, my written questions; then again, you answered them all.

And so I am and will remain

Your daughter,

Carol Ann

CHAPTER NINE

Controlling Fear and Its Goblins

"We can easily forgive a child who is afraid of the dark; the real tragedy of life is when adults are afraid of the light."
—Plato

Years ago a friend described her mother to me as someone who did almost nothing with her days because she was afraid of so many things. She couldn't fly to see her relatives in Michigan because she was afraid that her plane would crash. She could not drive to the grocery store because she was afraid of being killed in traffic. She could not walk around the block because she was afraid of falling and breaking her hip. She could not eat at a restaurant for fear of catching a disease from food served in a public place. She kept her draperies closed tight because strangers passing by scared her. She kept her windows shut because the sound of cats meowing made her skin crawl. She kept her doors locked because people of different color and teenagers with spiked hair petrified her. Fear controlled her and kept her from living a rich, full life. It boxed her into an existence with no depth or breath, no excitement or challenge, no growth or fun.

The vision of this woman living such a frightened existence slipped into my mind as if slipping into one of the red folders in my file cabinet where I store items I want to be reminded of often.

As my friend went on to tell me more about her mother, I vowed to use this story of one person's life as a foil against which to pattern mine. Ever since hearing about the frightened woman, I have aimed my sights upon fears as they've bounced into my life. I tackle things that scare me with a full nelson before they wrap their arms around my psyche and flatten it to the floor. I believe as Virginia said in *The Hours* by Michael Cunningham, "Better, really, to face the fin in the water than to live in hiding."

A bigger than usual fear popped into my life several years ago. It wasn't turning fifty that hit me in the back of the knees. It was a friend's invitation to join a group of women on a trip to Italy. Odd though it may seem, my response to the invitation was, "What? I can't travel for two weeks without my husband. I don't speak Italian. I've never gone to a foreign country without my family. And this isn't even a tour. It's just a group of women who are going to wander idly around Tuscany and thereabouts." The whole adventure was much too loose. I was scared and couldn't sleep at night contemplating the vague threats that hovered around the notion of traveling in a strange place with people I barely knew.

"No thanks," I told my friend. But I called my travel agent and reserved my airline tickets. One part of me quivered with the notion of being "on my own" in a land where ordering from a menu or filling the car with gas would be like doing *The New York Times* crossword in pen and without a dictionary. But the other part of me cheered from behind: "Go, go, quickly before this fear multiplies like a virus." I could not allow a nebulous discomfort to get in the way of what might be a once-in-a-lifetime opportunity. I had to be bigger than my uncertainty.

As it turned out, taking this fear by the horns turned into one of the most exciting trips of my life. The two weeks in Italy taught me the joy of getting lost and, in the process, discovering far greater adventure than anything we had planned. It taught me the pleasure of allowing a day to unfold rather than holding tight to a schedule. It reminded me to watch for and enjoy the unexpected rather than being dismayed when it happens. The trip that so frightened me at the start led to the beginning of an Italian import business and to several additional trips to colorful, romantic Italy.

> *"Come to the edge," He said.*
> *They said, "We are afraid."*
> *"Come to the edge," He said.*
> *They came.*
> *He pushed them . . . and they flew.*
> —Guillaume Apollinaire

Some fears are merely misty blankets of discomfort that grow out of experience or lack of it. Others are a valid hint that real danger is near. It is logical to fear rattlesnakes when trimming ground cover on a Tucson spring morning. But is it logical to fear flying or bridges or high places or getting lost or making mistakes? Fear can inform us that danger lurks, but sometimes the things we fear have no logical basis.

We are conditioned to fear as we grow through childhood. Our friends, families, adversaries, and storybooks warn us about the many things that might hurt us, overtake us, embarrass us, give us pain, make us weak, and cause us grief. The list of monsters and scary magicians increases as we read newspapers, go to movies, and listen to stories at the water cooler or over the backyard fence about what happened around the corner or across the street. Just the other day I heard a news story about an abduction and murder of a young woman in our town. It was a wretched event, a heartbreaking story. The next morning I felt uncomfortable running at dawn along the riverbed a few miles from my home as I have been doing for the six years I've lived in Tucson. Does this mean I shouldn't run at the river or at dawn any longer? Does it mean I should give up running altogether? No. It just means that I will be more aware of what is happening around me than I was before I heard the news story. I won't, however, allow the sad event to send me into hiding.

Balance is key to dealing with our fears. Uncontrolled fear, like uncontrolled anger or sadness, can lead to ill health, suffering, and diminished quality of life. Each of our fears is a response that has been conditioned by something we've been taught, something we've experienced, or something we've heard, read, or seen. We respond to a stimulus in our own personal fashion, and as we do, we write an internal story about the stimulus and response that becomes part of our emotional history. Next time we confront the same stimulus, our fear is greater or lesser according to the story we have written about the event.

Say, for instance, that you are biking down a country road and a dog dashes from behind a tree and runs toward you, teeth bared and barking. How would you respond? Since my husband and I used to bicycle in the farm country outside of Columbus, Ohio, we often faced such an experience. Our reactions were a study. My husband would bare his teeth back at the dog, slow his pace, yell and scream at the mutt, sometimes throw rocks in its direction. He reacted as he did because he had grown up with a yippy, miniature French poodle that he never learned to love. Later he had experienced my being attacked by a German shepherd while running one morning. So, when we were together biking, he felt as though he needed to protect me. He didn't know whether this dog would attack one of us or both of us. He didn't know whether an electric fence circled the property. He didn't know whether the owners would emerge from the barn to call back their protector, so he reacted with sound and fury.

To compare, I was scared speechless every time I faced a charging beast. Besides having been bitten by a dog, the only other experience I had had with these pets occurred when I was young enough to play with dolls. My folks purchased a boxer they called Foley. The name was auspicious. Foley was wild. He ran away over and over again, and I remember my mother's distress at having to leave three small children alone while she ran round and round the neighborhood trying to retrieve their too-expensive, purebred investment. Foley turned furniture into shredded dog beds. He sharpened his teeth on my dolls and their wardrobes. He gnawed on the legs of our prized baby grand piano. I recall that he remained with us only long enough to leave a permanent scar on the place inside of me that in other children is the seat of animal love.

So years later, whenever a dog charged my bicycle, I moved into high gear. I was too frightened to spend any time watching what took place between my screaming husband and the animal. All I knew was to speed up as fast as my legs would allow, face forward, and concentrate on biking out of sight and sound of the sharp-toothed monster.

Now, if we had been bicycling with my sister, there is no doubt that she would have pulled up short, dismounted, and greeted the dog with a smile and some stroking of its jowls. She would have met its owners and inquired about the breeding of the pet and about the crops in the field behind the house. She would have been invited into the house for chocolate chip cookies fresh from the oven, plus a cold glass of milk. And she, no doubt, would have ended up buying one of the dog's offspring.

Take fifty people, put them in one scary situation, and watch as each reacts in his or her own, private way to what is happening. The reactions are diverse because each is connected to and colored by what went before in the person's life and to what lessons were learned through experience or teachings.

Exercise: Put Your Fear Factor Into Perspective

"What is needed, rather than running away or controlling or suppressing or any other resistance, is understanding fear; that means, watch it, learn about it, come directly into contact with it. We are to learn about fear, not how to escape from it."
—Jiddu Krishnamurti

Scary things happen. You feel frightened. And what do you do? In the following exercises, you will examine your attitudes about fear. You will list the types of fear that you carry inside. You will take a look at whether your fears are well grounded, and you will assess whether the way you react to fearful situations works for or against you.

By writing letters to the fears that affect your life, you will face your emotion and, rather than closing down because of fright, you will learn to recondition your reaction so it better suits your life. Instead of turning your back and running breathlessly from whatever frightens you, you will breathe deeply, look deliberately at your fear, and examine the situation to see what both it and your reaction to it have to teach you.

Nudge 1

Today you will begin to examine your fears with the goal of eventually determining (1) how fear affects the quality of your life, and (2) which of your fears are well-founded. To start, make a list of your fears. Next to each fear note where it originated. Are you afraid of snakes because your big brother hid one in your bed when you were ten? Or because your parents were afraid of reptiles? Or because you fear touching a slimy, slithery, possibly poisonous animal?

Do you fear making mistakes and looking stupid because your family made a habit of talking about how your big sister was the sibling with the brains? Or because your third-grade teacher made you sit on the floor in the hallway when you didn't pass your semester spelling test?

Are you afraid that your spouse will leave you because his love feels conditional, because your father left your mother when you were a child, or for some other reason? Are you afraid of contracting a serious disease because last week's news reported an outbreak of rare virus in Africa or because several of your relatives died from similar causes?

Define each of your fears and its contributing factor. Work on your list for at least twenty minutes. Include tiny fears and huge ones. Include fears that seem silly and those that practically send you into hiding. Do not censor. List each and every one of the fears that come to mind—the dentist, spiders, your children making it on their own, thunderstorms, strangers, death, odd-tasting foods, old age, loved ones suffering, loneliness, loss of hearing or sight, losing a friend or relative. Going through this process is like having an X ray taken of the fears that hide within every inch of your body.

Nudge 2

Now it is time to measure the weight of your fears. Look at your list and number the ten largest fears and the ten smallest fears. Choose one of the small, insignificant fears on your list, and write a letter to it, explaining when, where, and how the fear came to live with you. Did it spring out of a story you read, out of something you learned at home or school, or from a life experience? Explain to the fear what it means to have it as a companion that goes everywhere with you, that is with you whenever and wherever you eat, sleep, walk, and talk. Describe the size of the fear, the color, and the weight. Tell the fear how you would feel if you were able to remove it from your spirit and bury it in a small hole in the backyard, for good, forever.

In your letter answer the following questions:

- Are you bigger than this fear?
- Who is stronger? You or your fear?
- What is the worst that would happen if this feared thing/event came true, or didn't go away, or grew larger?
- If this thing/event happened, how do you think you would react? How would you react and what would you do if you controlled this fear?

Marie Curie said, "Nothing in life is to be feared. It is only to be understood." Do you believe that this is true about the small fear to which you have written today? Is there a way to understand this fear and then to live with it as a teacher rather than a foe? If so, explain how you understand the fear better today than you did yesterday. Explain how you feel differently about it and how your new understanding will make a difference in your life.

Nudge 3

Today you will choose a large fear from your list and slowly and deliberately dissect it to learn how it works, where it was born, what feeds it, and how it affects your life. You will look at it from many angles and cut into its core to learn what makes it tick and what connects it to your emotional heart.

Begin your letter to a significant fear after considering the following questions:

- Where are you, what is happening to you, and what are you doing when your fear surfaces?
- How do you feel when confronted by the person, event, or thought that frightens you? Weak? Breathless? Sweaty? Helpless? Childlike? Monstrous? How do you react to this confrontation?
- How often does fear surface?
- Do you react in the same way and think the same thoughts every time the fear arises? What are the thoughts that accompany this fear? How does your body react?
- What events, people, or memories from childhood are connected to this fear?
- Is another fear connected to the one you are writing about today? A fear from the past or a fear about something that could happen in the future? If so, what is it and how is it related to your large fear?
- What is the worst that could happen if your fear grew or materialized? How would it affect your life and the lives of those closest to you?

Addressing some or all of these questions in your letter will help you zip your fear open and peer inside. It will help you see what other fears feed this one, and what past circumstances and current memories preserve the power and impact of this emotion. Just as the mystery of a magic trick is lost once you learn its secrets, so too will the mists around your fear lift and drift away as you throw light and clarity onto the many bits and pieces that combine to give it life. As Livy said, "We fear things in proportion to our ignorance of them." By dissecting your fear, you will increase your knowledge, your confidence, and your ability to squeeze the power out of your fear.

SAMPLE LETTER: FROM DIANAH FORESTER, NEW HAVEN, CONNECTICUT.

My dear,

My fear is big today. I face the dark side of myself and it won't go away. It's the bitterness and anger that I thought I'd conquered that now seep up from between some unexpected cracks and stain my heart, my thoughts, and my ways. I think I'm over being hurt by the divorce process. I think I am ready to go on, leaving what's behind, behind. I think I AM going on. But NO! While I am going through this incredible learning process of living on my own, preparing to begin work outside the house again, raising children by myself, and getting my finances in order, while being helped by loving family and friends, I'm filled with the ugly bile of loathing for a man who so betrayed me while he was, at the same time, belittling me for not trusting him more with the matters of settling "our" affairs. How could he have done that? I want to lash out at him. Even though he no longer loves me, is he so callous that he can't eek out a word of acknowledgment for the care I am giving daily to our children, care that frees him to go on with his life unfettered by such concerns?

I fear what's wrong with me that I allow these thoughts and feelings to surface and resurface. Why can't I let them go? In part, my choices helped to create this monster mood of mine. I know that. Still the anger is very much there and I fear I cannot shake the negative side of me. I desire to rise above down feelings. I want to use my time productively, joyfully, well. I'm disappointed by my own crummy attitude, my short temper with the children, my thoughts clouding what could be hours of joy.

I keep saying to myself, "This is MY life now. I don't have to let him in." Much of the time, that works. But oh, those hours when it doesn't, it really doesn't. I stew in waves of self-pity, feeling like there's no getting to the top again. It scares me because I almost revel in my hate and anger. I see myself doing this and am ashamed at a weakness which, when I see it in others, I forgive as being human.

But then, I write to myself, to the Universe that guards and takes care of me. I know I can wail and be heard. I know I can celebrate with wine and chocolate. I know that a good sleep will help immensely. It's a triumph when I am again in control and on top, and I get there, but my ugly side lurks. It haunts me from a place I haven't yet been able to cleanse. It's there, a shameful pain that I fear like a child fears the devil.

Nudge 4

"Courage is not the absence of fear, but rather the judgment that something else is more important than fear."
—Ambrose Redmoon

Often we avoid tackling our fears until we realize they are keeping us from doing or being something we desire. For instance, if you hate to travel, a fear of flying presents no problem. If you never get ill, the fear of doctors' offices has no bearing in your life. If you never enter a tall building, a fear of elevators is inconsequential. But let's say your daughter and son-in-law move across the country and are about to have their first child. Sitting in an airplane for five hours is beyond what you think you can handle, but you want desperately to help your daughter when she leaves the hospital and you want to hold your first grandchild in your arms. What do you do? Miss out on both precious experiences? Probably not, because being with your family becomes more important than your fear. Seeing your daughter as a mother for the first time becomes your focus. Through writing letters to your fear, through visualizing yourself walking on and off the plane safely, through practicing deep breathing techniques and focusing on the hours you will spend rocking your new grandchild to sleep, you are able to replace your fear with activities that enrich your life experience.

Write a new letter to the fear you addressed in Nudge 3 (page 163), or choose another major fear and write to it. Discuss the things your fear has prevented you from doing or accomplishing. Picture yourself grabbing hold of your fear, taking charge, and doing whatever it is you fear. Describe this action in writing, being as detailed as you can about where you are, what you are doing, who you are with, and how you feel and look as a result of beating back your fear. Describe how you feel as you accomplish the things your fear has prevented you from doing in the past. Do you feel happy, strong, nurtured, inspired, and confident in yourself and your ability to learn and grow?

Write and write as if you are doing what you have wanted or

needed to do but were afraid you could not. Write and write until the vision of your fear fades into the shadow of the clear, bright image of the event or achievement that is more important to you.

SAMPLE LETTER: FROM JENNIFER JOHNSON OF SANTA CLARA, CALIFORNIA, WHO SAYS, "I DIDN'T EXPECT THE LETTER THAT CAME WHEN I SAT DOWN TO WRITE IT; I HADN'T REALIZED BEFORE THAT MY GREATEST FEAR WAS PART OF MYSELF, MUCH LESS THAT PART OF MYSELF THAT I'VE IDENTIFIED MOST CLOSELY WITH MY WRITING."

Dear Lilith,

It's been a while, hasn't it? I've been ignoring you again, locking you away in your room in the recesses of my mind. I've heard you pounding on the door; you're loudest when I try to write. But I also hear you in the night when I can't sleep. I hear you when I'm scrubbing the tub, or baking bread. Sometimes you tap gently; sometimes you hammer so hard your knuckles must be bruised. I'm not ready to let you out, but we both know I can't continue this. You always escape, skipping away as my racing heart tries to catch you. For now, it's safest to write this letter and slip it under the door. Maybe it will stop your pounding and let my heart beat quietly today. So I'm writing to you, writing with another morning's chill in the air, writing with a lawn mower's low growl like a threatened animal in the distance.

Do you remember when I conjured you from the shadows of my mind, christening you after the woman who came before Eve? As I sat in that apartment with its yellow walls and dirt-colored carpet, I saw your indigo eyes and dark, tangled hair. You wore a blue dress, like Miranda in the

Waterhouse painting. You appeared because I needed to write but didn't think I could. I named you Lilith because she knew what it meant to leave home and wander the world, alone. She was powerful; she didn't just follow the rules. I wanted to be like her—strong enough to make my own story. So my imagination formed you. I called you, asked you to help me write, to help me right things through my writing.

Now I imagine you with dark circles under your eyes and skin so pale I see the blue of your veins. Now you can terrify me. You've given me life through writing, but at a cost. I should have read Rumi sooner. He said, "The images we invent could change into wild beasts and tear us to pieces." I hear the snarling of the lawn mower this morning and think of that, of how you have tried to tear me into pieces.

I often feel crazy when I think of you, as if I were a split personality, truly torn apart. I'm not; you are me. You are who I am when I create, but you are also a destructive force in me that I cannot always control. Whenever I write, I fear what you'll say—what I'll say—if I'm utterly honest. I fear your criticism and its consequences. I know you've helped me tap something true and deep and mystical. But you've also made me grind my teeth at night and spend day after day in bed, dull to the world, wrapped in a woolen blanket of depression. You tell me I'm not worth your time. When I let you roam free in my mind, you mutter, "You're not good enough. Nothing you write will ever be good enough." So I lock you away. I'm tired, Lilith, tired of feeling that every time I try to write I must jam my fingers in my ears against your mutterings. Stop trying to convince me that despair or madness is the price I must pay to be a writer.

Surely not all of us must live—and die—in that bell jar. Yet what else is there in life but creation and destruction, dancing?

I wish that I really could dance with you, Lilith, that I could grab your cold hands and whirl you around my living room, laughing. I think it would do us both good to get a little dizzy. When we were done, we could hug like old friends and sit on the porch for a while with the sun on our faces, talking about what I want to write. But in order to do that I'd need to let you out of your room and listen to you, wouldn't I? What would happen if I did? I'd either write or die trying. And if I didn't? I'd die without writing.

Sounds dramatic, but that's what I fear. Death. Like Sylvia. Write or die. But then I realize: It is my choice to make. I imagine you reading this letter and unlocking your door. You had the key all along, didn't you? Maybe your knocking was a rhythm we could dance to after all. I take a deep breath. We sit down together to write; I sit down to write. The lawn mower has stopped growling. I find words, and I find there is joy here, no need for fear. I find I can be a woman, a writer, a single soul in love with life and language.

Love, Eve

Nudge 5

Eleanor Roosevelt said, "We gain strength, and courage, and confidence by each experience in which we really stop to look fear in the face . . . we must do that which we think we cannot."

Now that you have grown to be larger and stronger than your greatest fear, write a letter to it describing how good you feel. Pretend for a moment that you are ten years old, and draw a picture of you and your fear at the top of your letter. Draw yourself twice the size of your fear. Draw yourself wringing the power out of your fear, stamping your fear flat, or putting your fear in a red helium balloon that goes up, up, up, and away. Have fun with your drawing as you slip back into the mind-set of a child who can imagine having great strength and ability. Be Superman or Superwoman. Put on your magic cape, fly out of reach of your fear, fling your fear up into the universe, way beyond the sun, beyond Jupiter, beyond the Milky Way.

You are positive. You are strong. You hold insights about your fear that you lacked a week ago, insights that give you new strength and power. Tell your fear about this new you. Put your fear in its place and walk away.

In this final step of saying good-bye to your fear, draw one more picture—a simple, iconlike picture of your fear. Then, either burn or bury the drawing as a way of totally ending your relationship with your fear. During the ceremony congratulate yourself for sticking with this difficult assignment, and go away contemplating the words of Jiddu Krishnamurti: "What is needed, rather than running away or controlling or suppressing or any other resistance, is understanding fear; that means, watch it, learn about it, come directly into contact with it. We are to learn about fear, not how to escape from it."

CHAPTER TEN

Examining Your Pain and Moving Forward

"Your pain is the breaking of the shell that encloses your under-standing. Even as the stone of the fruit must break, that its heart may stand in the sun, so must you know pain. And could you keep your heart in wonder at the daily miracles of your life, your pain would not seem less wondrous than your joy. And you would accept the seasons of your heart, even as you have always accepted the seasons that pass over your fields. And you would watch with seren-ity through the winters of your grief."
—Kahlil Gibran, *The Prophet*

Nighttime is quiet with its peaceful release and refresh-ment—sometimes. Sometimes it's not so quiet when the pain of worry, sadness, loss, confusion, or disappointment rears its ugly head. The pain that hides during daytime under a blanket of busyness sometimes arises to prance through the wee hours like a bristly, little monster screeching round a maypole.

In the middle of the day, I can manage emotional pain by intel-lectually compartmentalizing it as one of the seasons of my heart. To me, looking at life's hurt this way is comforting, for I can see pain as a cycle that will eventually evolve into something else and that has lessons to teach if I pay attention. But at night, halfway between dusk and dawn, pain does not yield to my rational thinking. I lie awake aching over the operation my father faces for removal of a tumor. My body and mind cramp with news of my son's apartment being burglarized, his car stolen. My teeth clench with the fright of my daughter attempting in her social work occupation to help young people survive in inner-city Chicago. Mistakes I made years ago poke their thorny heads into my sleepy shoulders and cause me to toss and turn.

I fight back by trying to concentrate on something else—on my breath, for instance, or on the space between my eyes. I try to shift my thinking by imagining my body relaxing, muscle by muscle from head to toe. I remind myself that allowing painful thoughts and feelings to rule the night does me no good. Round and round I roll with negative emotions until I grow too weary for further battle and slide peacefully back into sleep.

Pain is as natural as happiness in life. Intellectually I know that rejection, failure, loneliness, insecurity, heartache, and sadness cycle through our days not because we deserve them, not because we earn or invite them, but just because life is a complicated quilt of challenge and peace. But when the painful things happen, my emotional self feels surprised and wants to run and hide. I don't read the daily newspaper and do not watch the five o'clock television reports because I'd rather not carry around the pain that pours into my psyche from the media. But there it is—suffering in faces on the magazine covers at the checkout line, sadness in the stories friends tell me about failing health and crumbling relationships, personal pain that shakes me awake in the middle of the night.

Pain surrounds us whether we choose to look it in the face or not. But how do we talk about it and deal with it? How do you tell your spouse how you felt when your doctor found a spot on your X ray or when you were suddenly downsized out of a job?

Try to define your own feelings or comprehend your daughter's when her husband leaves to be with another woman. We can see pain in a brother's tears, in the droop of a mother's shoulders, or in the heaviness of a daughter's movements. We can hear pain in a friend's tone of voice and in the wail of a mourner's cry. But how do we put words to what we feel when in the grip of a painful experience? And what do we do to get through the agony?

I believe there is something to be learned from watching men and women who engage in extreme physical challenges and rise above the discomfort by relying on the power of their thoughts. Take, for instance, the triathletes who tackle the Hawaiian Ironman contest. Or, the athlete whose nickname is "King of Pain"— John Stamstad, an ultramarathon mountain biker who won a one hundred-mile race after breaking his collarbone in a fall at the twenty-mile mark. Why anyone would choose to endure such physical misery is a mystery. But the point is, Ironman contestants, John, and many other athletes succeed because they accept pain as normal, learn to handle it by shifting their thinking about it, and often use the pain to their advantage.

Physical pain, emotional pain, and thought mesh together into a complex web. We experience something emotionally painful and feel pressure at the center of our chests. Our stomachs flip-flop. We feel weary, slow, empty, and achy. We become foggy, confused, disoriented, uninterested. The emotional baggage connected to a painful experience is heavy. It is insistent, beating against us like tidal waves pounding the shore. It rips our heart in two and screams inside of us for release.

Our bodies react when something emotionally painful happens. Our minds do, too, connecting the experience with memories of previous events and filtering it through our belief system, our sense of self, and our strengths and weaknesses. Eventually the experience evolves into a collection of thoughts and memories we harbor about what happened. And yet through the process, we cannot see, show, nor measure what is happening. We deal with pain as we experience the wind by watching a tree bend and sway.

So, with a phenomenon that we have no difficulty feeling but great difficulty putting into words, how do we deal with emotional pain? How do we share what we are going through with someone else? What do we do about emotional pain when it happens? Can we learn by watching extreme athletes who accept pain as inevitable in life and who do not give in to it?

In this chapter's exercises, you are going to act like a winning athlete who overcomes pain by thinking about it in a new way. You are going to redefine emotional pain as a natural process of life that is temporary and manageable. Like an experienced athlete, you will examine your emotional pain, pay attention to it, and move through it to knowledge, release, and comfort.

Exercise 1: *Which Hurts Slide Right Off Your Shoulders?*

While researching the nature of pain, I read an article that described neural circuits that suppress the pain of wounds. The circuits are thought to have evolved to aid animals in defending themselves during attack and in escaping further harm. As I read about this aspect of the pain phenomenon, I thought about how much of the discomfort that comes our way slides right off of our shoulders. We could not possibly weigh, consider, digest, and carry with us every painful happening that walks into our lives. For instance, consider an afternoon of doing errands. You shop for annuals for your garden, stop at the post office to mail a package, and visit the service station for a lube and oil change. If you took to heart every rude and thoughtless gesture that came your way during these hours, you would never leave home again. If your feelings were hurt every time someone treated you harshly, said something hurtful, arrived late for an appointment, or forgot to do for you what they said they would, you would constantly feel disappointed, saddened, and pained by life.

In the following nudges, you will consider your ability to ignore some of the hurts that wash through your life. You will examine why it is that some experiences bring pain while others do not. You will explore the notion that our thoughts cause us to hurt in some instances and not in others. And, you will practice rewriting painful stories into less painful dialogue.

Nudge 1

Draw a line across the center of a page of paper. Below that line list as many recent experiences as you can remember that could have been hurtful but that your defense system allowed you to toss aside. What about a friend's thoughtless comments that you ignored because they weren't worth notice? What about rude treatment of clerks, teachers, people on the road, your children, or your parents that could have crushed you but that you let fade away? List as many events as come to mind. Add to the list as more of these slight irritations happen.

Above the line list several big hurts, ones that sank into your heart and gnawed at your innards. List enough of these to get a sense of the sorts of events that matter enough to get under your skin.

Now write a letter to yourself describing why the line exists where it does between hurts that you allow to evaporate and hurts that you cannot forget. Compare one of the potentially painful experiences that you let fade away (one below the line) with one that landed squarely in your heart (one above the line).

- How did the two events differ?
- How did your emotional and physical reactions to the two events differ? When you think about the two events today, do you feel any physical or emotional pain connected to either one?
- Why or how were you able to let go of the one and not the other?
- How long ago did each of these events happen?
- How long do you usually remember and hold on to hurtful events?
- Do you think it possible to increase your capacity to let pain slide off your shoulders and to shift the line so that fewer and fewer things cause you discomfort? If so, how do you plan to do this?

Nudge 2

Pretend that one of the small painful memories that lingers in your heart is connected to a place. It could be a rock in your backyard where you sit now and then, a favorite chair in your home, a shady spot under a tree in the park, or the corner booth at a coffeehouse you sometimes visit. Mentally visit your pain in that location. See yourself sitting in the spot, enveloped by the cloud of your pain.

Now, in a letter to this spot that represents your pain, carefully describe what you are feeling.

- Is it betrayal, dishonesty, thoughtlessness, neglect, distrust, disappointment, imperfection, or something else tied to the hurtful event?

- Is your pain less now than it was when the hurtful event happened? Do all of your hurts fade over time, or do you hold on to some, not wanting or able to let them go?
- Why do you think you have held on to this pain for more than a moment? Has holding on to it helped you *not* feel or remember some other hurt? Have you held on to it because of a belief? An insecurity? A resentment? A wish? If so, what is it?
- Do you want to get rid of this pain? Or does it feel good or useful (in getting attention or sympathy) to harbor it?

As you name and write about what you feel concerning the painful event, imagine yourself standing up and walking away from the place that symbolizes your pain. See yourself walking out of and away from the cloud of hurt. Describe in writing the feeling of leaving the hurt behind, where it will gradually evaporate like dew from green grass on a spring morning. Describe what you have learned about yourself by visiting with and carefully looking at this small hurt, lessons that you might be able to use when facing larger hurts.

SAMPLE LETTER: FROM KIM SANWALD-REIMANIS, KALAMAZOO, MICHIGAN. "I HAVE LEARNED THAT LETTER WRITING IS NOT ABOUT CONTROL OR BEING CAREFUL, BUT IS A JOURNEY OF PERSISTENCE, PATIENCE, AND FORGIVENESS, DURING WHICH WE FORGE NEW MEANINGS BY SLOWING DOWN AND SAVORING OUR RELATIONSHIPS AS THEY UNFOLD," SAYS KIM. "I WROTE THE FOLLOWING LETTER AND THEN READ IT AT MY MOTHER'S GRAVE SITE ON MOTHER'S DAY."

Dear Mom,

Another Mother's Day approaches and I find myself staring out my living room window. Pink, yellow, and white hyacinth bloom with brilliance along our sidewalk. I smile and receive spring's promise of rebirth.

Seven years have passed since your death and I sense a deep change occurring within. Although physically gone, you continue to be a presence in my life. I see you in unexpected glimpses through my relationship with others. Sometimes these reminders come unwelcome. Other times they tug at my heart. Always they provide meaningful lessons. Our parting sent me on a journey of forgiveness and responsibility. I have prayed for clarity to understand and transcend my pain. I have harnessed the stubborn tenacity I learned from your example to chart a different course for myself.

Now, rather than wall myself from our similarities, I welcome them. I applaud my directness and feel free to speak my mind. I am learning to temper my bluntness by being respectful of others. Rather than let my fears control me and intimidate those around me, I use fear as a signpost to dig deeper in the understanding of myself.

My pain has taught me empathy and compassion for others in their life struggles. My isolation and depression have allowed me to embrace solitude as a teacher. I find myself thirsty for life, the moisture of which swells my heart, as each drop finds me, until I am drenched and laughing. Joseph Campbell said, "Find a place where there is joy and the joy will burn out the pain."

How important to let love in. It shatters all our old boundaries and rigidities. It allows Mystery to be what it is. The Mystery of Love changes lives forever. When our paths cross again I'm sure my soul will recognize the light within you.

How do I explain to you what you and our relationship have meant to me? I have written many letters to others with my heart spread all over them, and not once have I tried to convey to you how deeply you reside there. Love cannot be held back and still called love. Love is not about being careful, rationing it out like a miser counts coins. In order for it to survive, it must be given and given freely.

I acknowledge our deep love for each other, which was continually challenged by our similarities and passions. Rage, left unchecked, can be so unsympathetic. Though I am not a parent, I am a woman who nurtures both myself and others with great tenderness. I continue to be a work in progress. I am learning a love that tempers my judgments and opens my heart. I am keenly aware that before my soul can rest, I must accept your flaws as my own and hold them tenderly. They have been your greatest gifts.

When I look in the mirror and see your face, my eyes soften, and I see your secret poetry. I cannot forget you. Alice Walker said, "In search of my mother's garden I found my own." Much love,
Kim

Exercise 2: Now for the Major Hurts

"Individuals behave, not in accordance with reality, but in accordance with their perception of reality. How the individual feels about himself or herself is everything, for all that he or she ever does or aspires to do will be predicated on that all-important concept which is the self-image."
—Dr. Denis Waitley, *The Psychology of Winning*

Thinking about Dr. Waitley's premise, you are going to write several letters about one of your biggest hurts. You will choose an emotionally painful experience that haunts you and write to this hurt from your own viewpoint, from that of an "emotion coach," and from that of a longtime friend. By doing so you will use role-playing to expand your reality. It will be like changing your vision from normal to wide-angle.

After you experiment with looking at yourself in a painful experience through several sets of eyes, you will ask yourself whether your way of dealing with hurt works for or against you. You will have the opportunity to redefine your experience of pain if you decide that doing so would help you move more gracefully through hurtful seasons of life.

Before you begin, think about the power of your belief system. If you see the world as a kind and gentle place, you react differently to cruelty than if you believe that life is a game of survival of the fittest. If you believe that through suffering you earn a place in heaven, you react differently to what comes your way than if you believe that reward and meaning come with rejoicing in life. If you believe that all things are connected, you react differently to events than if you see yourself as a separate, totally self-actualized individual.

Our thoughts determine our actions. And since our thoughts can be changed, so can our reactions to hurtful events. Think about the power of your beliefs and about the power you have to alter them as you work on your next few letters.

Nudge 1
Write a letter to one of your major hurts as if it were a person, animal, hour, or object. Name your hurt to get into the game of

seeing it as an entity. Beginning your letter, for instance, "Dear Day when Betty turned her back on me," will give solid form to your hurt. It will allow you to walk around the pain, grab hold of it, and sit down with it for serious discussion.

Addressing the person or thing you have chosen to symbolize your painful experience, define what the experience was and when it occurred. Tell who was involved and how your feelings and physical reaction connected with the event have changed over time. Describe the questions that still remain concerning the event. Explain what you have learned since the event happened that has helped ease the pain.

Continue your letter by addressing some of the following questions:

- What beliefs and past experiences color your perception of the hurtful event?
- When this painful event happened, did the pain connected with it determine when you got up in the morning or whether you were able to sleep at night? Have the emotional and physical pain connected to the event lessened over time? If so, how and why?
- Did the pain of this hurtful event determine who you spent time with and what you did during the day? Does it still?
- Did the pain keep you in a relationship, in a job, or in a circle of friends that you might not have chosen were it not for the emotion? Does your pain continue to affect you in the same way?
- Did your hurt affect the way you ate, exercised, dressed, and played? Does it still?
- What about your self-concept caused you to react to the painful event as you did? Would you like to have reacted in some other

way? Would you change any part of your self-concept if possible? If so, how?

SAMPLE LETTER: PATTI HAWN, MANHATTAN BEACH, CALIFORNIA, MADE A PAINFUL DECISION EARLY IN LIFE ABOUT THE ADOPTION OF HER SON. "I WROTE THIS LETTER SEVERAL YEARS PRIOR TO A REUNION WITH MY SON. I PETITIONED THE COURTS TO UNSEAL THE DOCUMENTS AND LEARNED HE WAS LIVING IN A HALFWAY HOUSE ON THE EAST COAST," SHE SAYS. "THE DEVELOPING RELATIONSHIP HAS BEEN A COMPELLING JOURNEY BEYOND THE PREDICTABLE."

Dear Son,

I said good-bye to you many years ago. You were small and helpless and so was I. It didn't seem like a very good match, so I did what seemed like a good idea at the time. I gave you away. I thought you would have a better chance in this life with two parents who were married, had a home, and could afford to give you the so-called advantages that were revered in the fifties. There was a lot of agreement for this decision at the time. My mother was a take-charge kind of lady who, when presented with a problem, took action. In this case, the action was adoption. I was told it would be selfish to consider anything else.

By the time the decision was made, I was actually feeling rather noble about my gift of you. I dropped out of school, created a past that included a husband, moved to Pittsburgh for seven months with a kind family member, and watched in awe as you grew inside my body. You and I spent many hours in the library, visiting exotic places and reading stories of people who became my friends and teachers. I always hoped you would like to read and learn.

I massaged your tiny knees and elbows as they rippled across my belly while you tried to find your spot inside of me. I watched in fascination as you changed my young girl's body into that of a woman. My breasts grew large and full in preparation for the milk that you never drank. I shared many secrets with you in those months. I told you that I would always be with you, even though you would not know it, and that each October 18 I would have a birthday party for you. I told you about your unique and talented family. Your southern grandfather, who played music for kings and presidents and could make a violin weep and a clarinet laugh, and your tiny Jewish grandmother, who was a master story-teller whose smile was so radiant and eyes so wise that she enchanted all who knew her.

I told you of your beautiful aunt who could hold an ara-besque longer than anyone in our dancing class and was just beginning an extraordinary journey that would lead her throughout the world and into the hearts of millions. I told you of the young boy who was your father. He had a kind laugh and a keen mind, and I knew he would grow up to be a hero and a scholar. And he did.

As for me, my favorite color is yellow. I will eat almost anything except raw oysters. I have always owned a dog and wouldn't live in a house without a fireplace. I love the sea but need to feel trees often. I don't like boats. Brazilian jazz makes my body move, and I can't imagine anything more thrilling than getting on a plane to visit somewhere I've never been. I have a husband who makes me laugh almost all of the time and two sons who constantly teach me about love.

There isn't much that scares me except the thought of never seeing you. I made a promise long ago to remain silent in your life, and I have for forty years. Now I break my silence and my promise. I want nothing from you but to look into your eyes, touch your face, and know that you are safe.
Patti

Nudge 2

Now write a letter to yourself about the hurtful event as if you are your "emotion coach." We all have emotion coaches inside of us, but often we ignore the voice of wisdom that tells us what to do, what not to do, how to react, and how to avoid reacting.

Since we often do not trust our own, inner direction, think of a coach, teacher, mentor, or counselor who once provided help when you needed it. Picture this person as you write today's letter, and think about how you would take to heart the advice of your coach if you were trying to win a swimming, biking, or debating championship.

Pretend you are the coach who watches the hurtful event unfold. Describe what you see happening. Describe the players involved, their demeanors, and their actions toward one another. Add information from the past that casts light on the situation. Interpret what is happening from your point of view. Make suggestions about how the players (you, especially) can handle the pain, move through it instead of getting mired down in sadness, and come home victorious. Suggest what might be learned from the situation so that similar events can be avoided in the future.

Have fun with this exercise. See what you can learn from giving free reign to the voices inside of you that know the truth of the situation.

Nudge 3

It's time now to write a letter about the same hurtful event from the eyes of a close, thoughtful friend. Visualize someone whose opinion you value, someone who is a good listener, who is honest, and who has known you and the other people in the situation for a long time. Crawl into the heart of this friend and write a letter to *you* describing the hurtful event. Through the friend's eyes, describe what you see, hear, and feel about the event. Throw light onto the situation from your friend's point of view. As the friend, make suggestions as to how *you* can survive the pain of this event and, in addition, grow wiser and stronger because of it.

While writing this letter, you may refer to actual thoughts, feelings, and advice that friends have shared with you about this hurtful event. Not all advice or every comment that comes to you from friends is useful. Not all of it feels good. But considering and responding to what others have said about the situation might tilt the event in just such a way that your vision of it becomes broader and deeper.

Nudge 4

Now that you've written letters from three different viewpoints about the same hurtful scenario, read your letters aloud. What was the tone of each letter? How did the tones and interpretations differ? Which letter feels most kind, wise, telling, honest? Which interpretation of the event is real? Are any of the interpretations *not* real?

Write a letter to yourself now, discussing your ability to deal with pain. Think for a moment of pain as the man in the moon. Some of us see the smiling face; some of us don't. But the disparity doesn't mean that some of us are right, some wrong. It only means that we interpret things differently.

As you write to yourself about how you deal with pain, think about the possibility of expanding your interpretation of one painful event in your life. Is it possible to see the face in the moon if you never have before, or to turn the face to the dark side if its smile haunts your dreams? Experiment with enlarging your story. Walk around the event to see it from different angles and during various seasons of life. Describe the event as it affects you on a gray, rainy day, and then describe it as it affects you on a sunny, Saturday afternoon. Talk to yourself about how you might "re-package" your memory of the painful event so that it causes you less hurt. Congratulate yourself for the effort you are putting into improving your well-being.

Continue to write to yourself about your emotional pain. As you become better at easing hurts connected to yesterday, your ability to apply this technique to today's painful events will improve, too. The will to survive and to be well is strong. As Helen Keller said, "Although the world is full of suffering, it is also full of the overcoming of it."

SAMPLE LETTER: FROM KATHERINE E. RABENAU, MESA, ARIZONA, WHO SAYS, "ALTHOUGH I EXPECTED AND GOT NO RESPONSE FROM SENDING THIS LETTER, WRITING IT WAS A FIRST STEP IN COMING TO GRIPS WITH MY PAIN AND GRIEF AT WHAT HAD HAPPENED."

November 11, 1988

Walter

Duchess County Jail
Poughkeepsie, New York
   Dear Walter:
Forty-one days ago, for reasons I suspect even you do not understand, you stabbed my sister to death in a grocery store parking lot. She was my big sister, part of my universe since the day I was born. I am the person that I am at least in part because of things she taught me and shared with me and did with me. I loved her very much and I wish you had not killed her.

I wish you could have known Carole, because she was a very kind and giving person. She cared about the world and the people in it, and she did what she could to make it a better place. And it is a better place for her having lived. She was the kind of person who would have hated what you've done, but she would not have hated you. She was better than hate. She was about love and life and being. She wasn't a saint and she wasn't perfect. She was just a good and kind person. She was worthy of a better death.

It's hard for me to understand what the world could have done to you that you would take a life under any circumstance, but especially for no reason at all. I mourn for my sister, and I worry about and grieve for the pain her death has brought her husband and children, my parents, my brother, and myself. It hurts more than I ever imagined possible.

But I want you to know, Walter, that I grieve for you, too. Not with the sharp, bleeding pain I feel about my sister. But it makes me so very sad to think that you can be alive and yet have a heart that is so apparently dead. Whatever life did to you to put you in such darkness is, on some level, the responsibility of every living soul. We have failed you, and you have failed us. A piece of everyone dies in such a death.

So, I want you to know that I pray for you. I hate what you did, and I doubt that I would like you very much if I were to meet you. But maybe, if my sister's death is to have some meaning, perhaps it will bring some light into your soul. Perhaps Carole's death was her final generosity; her life, to redeem something in yours. That's an extraordinary gift. I hope you don't waste it.

Sincerely,

Katherine E. Rabenau

CHAPTER ELEVEN

Sending a Letter as a Further Step in the Healing Process

"Twenty years from now you will be more disappointed by the things you didn't do than by the ones you did do. So throw off the bowlines. Sail away from the safe harbour. Catch the trade winds in your sails. Explore. Dream. Discover."
—Mark Twain

I have been studying yoga for about two years and am quite fascinated by what I call the release of the discipline. By that I mean the phenomenon that happens when I feel as though I've stretched as far as I can. I arrive at that position, breathe in fully and, as I exhale, my body sinks deeper into the stretch. Another inhale and exhale and my body sinks even deeper, without effort but with a mental letting go of the boundary between yes and no.

I see this release in yoga as a metaphor for our relationships with both ourselves and others. We arrive at points in our lives when we believe that we've gone as far as possible or have given as much as we're able to the people we love. We feel as though we've tried as hard as we can to clear up misunderstandings or to knock down walls of discomfort, disagreement, or discord that stand between ourselves and the people significant to us. We wake up one day feeling as though we have no more energy, we've hit the wall and have run out of ideas or out of desire. Then we take a deep breath, a time-out, another look, and we realize that we can, indeed, sink deeper into our commitment, our understanding, and our love for a person near and dear to us.

In writing letters for this final chapter, you will find that release plays a big part in the process. As you begin to write, you will feel as though a heavy anchor is being lifted and a gentle breeze is filling your sails. It is important to note here that although actually sending a letter is not a necessary step in the healing process, doing so may lead to the growth you desire.

The purpose behind writing letters for this chapter is to get to the core of the matter, to think a new thought, feel a new level of emotion, see an event with new eyes. It will not be enough to tell someone that you are angry, sad, confused, hurt, or deliriously happy. You already know that much, and the future recipient of your letter (if you decide that it's wise to send it) probably does, too. What you need to do is clarify why you feel as you do, why you've avoided writing the letter until now, what you would like to achieve by writing and possibly sending your letter, what you would like from the recipient if you send your letter, and what else you are willing to do to achieve the goal you've described.

We hold so many messages deep in our hearts. We hold them there, silent and secret, because we are busy or frightened of being sappy or misunderstood. We imagine hurtful consequences of sharing what we feel. And so we tighten our grips and close the door on what lies inside our hearts.

By now you have privately explored your feelings in letters written for earlier exercises in this book. You have discovered things about who you are and how you react to the world. You probably have been tempted to put a stamp on one of the letters you've written, and mail it. But sending a letter that you have feared dropping in the mail takes a lot of trust. It takes trust in the veracity of your feelings, in your ability to express yourself in a way that will be understood, and in the strength of your relationship. Once you pick up your pen to write a letter that has been haunting you, you've either gained the trust you need or decided that you'd rather move forward with uncertainty than sit on the sidelines and miss out on the dance.

In this final chapter, you will do a bit more emotional stretching. In the letters you write, you will have control of what you say and how you say it. But, if you decide to send one of your letters (and remember that your healing might be accomplished without doing so), you will not have control of the response that comes from sending your message. You may get no word in return, or you may receive a flood of communication that overwhelms you. Your letter may open new doors, or it may close the door tighter than it was before. The recipient of your letter may rejoice upon reading your words and reach out with open arms. On the other hand, he or she may lash out and then take three steps even farther away from you. The response is out of your hands.

In writing, and perhaps in deciding to send your letters, you merely follow your heart and, by doing so, attend to your inner peace. To continue doing so, you must remember that (1) any response is possible, (2) the recipient's reaction may not be what you expect or desire, and (3) it is not your responsibility to erase what you have said or to "make nice" if the recipient reacts negatively.

Life is both pain and pleasure. You cannot have one without the other. You cannot control the dance of life. This moment is yours, but the next is out of your grip. You can hold your emotions silent, or you can set your voice upon the wind, having faith that what your heart leads you to say is good, true, and worthy of being heard.

I suggest that you put on the music and dance. There's no guarantee where your steps will lead. You may write many letters and decide not to mail any of them, but dive into the process. In the act of writing, you will make discoveries and feel release. If that is enough, fine. Keep your letters in a locked drawer. If you decide to mail one of the letters, do so and feel confident that you have done your part and that the rest is up to the recipient. After all, that person is free to either join hands with you in the adventure of life or walk the other way, alone.

If the person to whom you write is no longer living or lost to you in some other way, you might choose to deliver the letter symbolically by burning it, burying it, or sharing it with someone who will listen, hear, and understand your gesture.

SAMPLE LETTER: FROM JIM EARLEY, MESILLA, NEW MEXICO.
For Professor Cousens, on the eve of your retirement:

When I entered the University of Puget Sound at eighteen in 1982, I knew only this: God had a plan for me. And if the unthinkable turned out to be true, that God did not exist and there really was no plan, I knew I'd better get the most out of college while I had the chance.

There was so much I did not know. I did not know for instance, what fraternities and sororities were, much less that half my dorm would be occupied by a secret society of young women identified by the wearing of sweatshirts emblazoned with three triangles. I did not know how to accept my body, which rheumatoid arthritis was conquering minute by minute. I did not know that I would join an ill-fated rock band, or that you, Professor Frank Cousens, were just around the corner.

By the second week of your English class, I was convinced you had to be the devil himself. Your daily ravings about the power of reason and the life of the mind rang blasphemously in my ears, and as I planned my rebuttals, which I kept to myself, something shocking happened. That voice telling me to open my mind to reason and critical judgment started to sound less like yours and more like my own.

Still, I was determined not to surrender quietly; that much I owed myself and my god. One day, well toward the end of a class during which your eyebrows had spent more time than ever arching above the rims of your glasses and your sentences had tumbled rapidly to their conclusions, my silence ended.

I can't remember if I raised my hand, but I do know that my voice gave out much sooner than I expected. I told you to stop criticizing Christianity all the time, and that my belief system was just as valid as yours was. As I prepared for ridicule, I sensed movement off to my side. A young woman who had never spoken before nodded her head in silent approval. Again, I waited.

"Perhaps you're right," you said. I searched for an indication that you did not mean it. I found none. "Perhaps you're right." And you dismissed class.

Much more happened to me while I was in college than your classes. I fell in love and found myself unable to handle it. I burned through three failed majors before deciding, reluctantly, on English. Gary Ong flung himself off the Narrows Bridge one night, prompting me to get drunk for the first time in my life and stumble around campus, grieving over a man I had barely known. A stand-up comedian mocked my appearance and my body mercilessly in front of hundreds of students as I sat stunned behind my drums waiting to play a set of rock and roll. But when I remember carefully what shifted the course of my life the most, I come back to you.

Why? You offered me what a seasoned tightrope walker offers an apprentice. You raised the thin cable higher and higher, and I, certain no net would catch me, plummeted wildly again and again. But the net was always there. By the next class period, I'd be eager to try again.

After graduating, I wanted to run from you, but with few prospects for work, I had to consider graduate school. My spotty literature background (I had focused mostly on professional and creative writing) left me pessimistic, but I plunged into the GREs, on which I performed unimpressively. You may remember that I asked you to send recommendations for me to three schools. Two rejected me. One, The University of Arizona, accepted me conditionally. I packed up and moved to Tucson.

My first visit to the campus, I met with the chair of graduate English to ask for clarification on my "conditional" status.

"Don't worry about that," he said. "We'll just have you audit a couple of undergraduate courses. By the way, I see that Frank Cousens thinks of you as quite the Conrad scholar."

I considered those words, Conrad scholar. If one two-page paper on *Nostromo* submitted to Frank Cousens qualified me as a Conrad scholar, then I suppose his statement had merit.

"I think you'll do just fine here," he said. "How is Frank? He caused quite a stir back in California."

That was the last I heard of my conditional status. I did

become somewhat of a Conrad scholar, but what I really discovered in graduate school was something even more unexpected. I discovered that I could convince people to walk the tightrope. I discovered that I was a teacher.

Now, I teach fulltime at a community college in New Mexico. As students stumble mentally bruised and intellectually battered through our open admissions door, I do what you taught me to do. I pamper that stubborn spark of confidence deep inside each student. Then I ask them all to come with me to the high wire. Learning in my class is not always pleasant, but it is always safe. I provide a net. One day, the students discover that they've been on the high wire for weeks, and they can't even remember when the net was removed.

Professor Cousens, you may be retiring, and that's a loss to us all. But your students are everywhere, and, in a way, so are you.

Yours,

Jim Earley

Writing a letter that you have been avoiding for whatever reason will require several rough drafts and may take a month or a year to complete. You will need to dig in your heels to figure out why you have put off writing this letter and what is at stake if you either write and send it . . . or avoid doing so forever. The process of putting words onto paper is not the difficult part. What causes the agony, promises the ecstasy, and takes the time is wiping the mystery off the face of your feelings. It is figuring out exactly why you feel angry, sad, disappointed, hurt, or ecstatic. But, as Mere Cunningham said about dancing, "The only way to do it is to do it."

I remember college English courses during which I felt as though I were having blood drawn every time I began to write an essay. That first sentence was a killer because it couldn't be written until I'd figured out what I wanted to say about the subject. After that, the rest was easy. Later, when I became an English teacher, it amazed me that so many of my students filled page after page with words without ever revealing what they thought, felt, or discovered about the subject. They didn't express it because they didn't take the time to think and feel. They were too busy filling up pages with words in an attempt to complete the assignment. If you were to write such a letter, the recipient would be as much in the dark about how you feel as you are.

Until now in this book, I have suggested that you let it rip as you write, that you do not censor, that you say it straight from your heart. Doing so has served you well in that you have been able to let go of emotions whose negative nature, at the very least, has kept you from being your best and, at the most, may have adversely affected your health.

Now, however, you have additional goals in mind. With a letter you plan to send, you may hope to heal an old hurt between you and a friend. You may hope to reestablish communication, set the record straight on your feelings concerning a misunderstanding, settle an old argument, or uncover a family secret. You may wish to tell someone how profoundly he or she has affected your life or how much you have missed with someone's absence. Your letter may be one of high praise or one of immense remorse. Whatever the emotion or goal behind your letter, you must first understand your purpose in writing and, next, choose words, phrases, examples, and tone that will work in your favor, not against it.

In the first chapter, I suggested that you give yourself time, privacy, and your version of silence to write. Remember this as you begin to compose a letter that calls to be written. Write a first draft one day, then read it aloud the next. Picture the recipient opening your message. In your mind's eye, watch for facial expressions and body language that reveal which words, phrases, or references in the letter fall gently on the recipient's ears and which fall like bricks and might be expressed another way without changing the essence of the message. I don't mean to suggest that you soft-pedal or avoid saying what needs to be said. I'm only suggesting that there are millions of ways to say something and that it will be in your best interest to express yourself in such a way that your message is heard and felt rather than thrown away partially read.

This final chapter is one of resolution. You have knocked down emotional roadblocks through writing unsent letters. You have brought clarity to issues in your life. Now it is time for the next step. Armed with new insight and self-confidence, you are ready to write the letters of praise and pleading that long to be shared. You are ready to write letters that rejoice the best of your relationships and letters that work toward mending those in need of repair. If you decide to include this final chapter in your healing process, it may lead to awakening for both you and the person to whom you write. Imagine the growth and renewal possible if, instead of remaining silent and distant because of a long-standing hurt, you explain in a letter to someone you love that you ache for something better between the two of you. Imagine the positive energy you send into another person's life every time you send a letter of thanks, appreciation, gratitude, or comfort.

The power of the pen is strong. Begin making use of its magic today. Be courageous. Open that box in your heart marked,

"Songs that need to be sung." Live fully, honestly, passionately. Pick up your pen and write, ecstasy, agony, and all.

Exercise: What Would You Say If . . .

We do a lot of putting off until later in our lives, not without good reasons. We're tired, not in the mood, frightened, confused, not ready, too busy. But what if you were running out of time or were allowed to write just one more letter or were promised that there would be no unpleasant consequences of sending a letter that you've wanted to write for a long time? Under these circumstances, what letter would you write? What would you say? How would it feel to send the letter?

More and more every day, I am reminded to live this day as if it were my last. Things that I see happening to people around me remind me that life is not only precious but fragile, too. If you wait until tomorrow to share what is in your heart, it may be too late.

For a few moments each day, pretend that this day is your last. Keep a running list of the letters you would send, the things you don't want to go unsaid. Then, one by one, write and send these letters. Our connection to one another is our definition. It is who we are, what we are. So pick up the pen and create yourself, in your own words, in your own way. The process promises only to make life richer and more meaningful.

Nudge 1

Search back through the unsent letters you've written and select one that calls out to be sent. Read your words aloud, and then write a letter to yourself explaining why you now want to send this letter. Do you want to make nice, cast blame, accept the problem as your own, clarify, heal wounds, reestablish contact, get even, praise, reveal long-held secrets, express gratitude, strengthen a relationship?

Spend at least twenty minutes writing to yourself. Don't hurry, for this is the time to define exactly what you hope to achieve by sending your message. What is your purpose? Remember that there is not a right and wrong reason to send a letter. But there is a need to know your purpose before rewriting and sending your message. As you explain your motives, include discussion about why you have put off writing this message until now and what has caused you to change your mind. Clarifying these issues will help you rewrite your letter with words and tone that work in your favor.

After finishing this message to yourself, begin the rewrite of your unsent letter. Pretend that this may be the last letter you send to the recipient. Use words, references, examples and tone that hit the mark but do not shatter the connection. After you've finished this first draft, do not send it. Let twenty-four hours pass. Read the letter aloud, slowly. Listen to your words. Feel their tone and effectiveness. Rewrite those parts of the letter that feel like scratchy wool on your back. Wait another twenty-four hours. Read your letter aloud. Repeat and repeat until your heart tells you the letter is ready. Then, send it feeling comfortable with the effort and sensitivity that went into its writing.

SAMPLE LETTER: FROM M. LEE KNIGHT, TUCSON, ARIZONA, WRITTEN AND THEN SENT AFTER MUCH DELIBERATION AND SOUL-SEARCHING.

December 7, 1989

Dear Dave,

After we left your home and our confrontation back in October, we did not know where to go. Don suggested a hotel, but I wanted to go home. I felt at that moment that I needed to be in our own place. But, by the time we reached Route 8, I'd changed my mind. I did not want to bring the highly charged discord of the previous days here, for that type of feeling has no place in our home of love and healing. So, we headed to the town of Alpine. What we sought was not there. On we went to Pine Valley where we stayed the night.

Amongst the pine forest, we found the balm our spirits needed. One cannot remain unsettled in such a setting, for there is little of man present, but much of God. Our healing began in the silence of that woodland. The next night, we stayed in Gila Bend and felt a little more peace of mind descend upon us. Though still puzzled as to the "why" of the confrontation that had taken place, we arrived home.

I have found over the years that nothing happens by chance. Although I may not be able to see the reason for a situation, there is always one, and something to learn, too. As I found my mind frequently drifting to our visit and felt unsettled reliving its vignettes, I asked for guidance just before sleep, as I am prone to do. I asked for clarity of thought and understanding, and a way to express my philosophy of life.

In the middle of the night, as often happens, I received the insights I longed for, and this is what came to me. I hold your right to be what your being dictates inviolable. But in exchange, friend, I claim the same. Our perceptions are different, since they are created by our unique experiences

and are colored according to our individuality. May we always, you and I, respect the rainbow of the other. It is not
for me to judge you, nor for you to judge me, for we are
each on our own right path, learning the lessons we need in
this lifetime.

I salute the path you have chosen, even as I cannot understand it. It is your way and not mine, just as my path is mine
alone and not yours. This is said in love and learning, with
a deep desire for the peace of spirit we all wish for yet seldom
attain.

Your mother-in-law,

Lee

Nudge 2

*"Perfection is achieved, not when there is nothing left to add, but
when there is nothing left to take away."*
—Antoine de St. Exupery

Choose another of your unsent letters. Until now you have refrained from sending this message. With this nudge you will examine why as you practice paring your message down to the essentials. Take twenty minutes to rewrite your letter as if you were
going to send it tomorrow morning. Don't hesitate, don't censor.
Write whatever thoughts come to you, but don't send the letter.
Read St. Exupery's quote, and set your letter aside for a day.

When you return to your letter, think about how few words a
poet uses to convey a message. How many words can you elimi-
nate while preserving the essence of what you want to say? Try
crossing out all of the adverbs in your letter. What happens to
the tone of your message? Is it weakened or strengthened? Pre-

tend that you have just one page or one paragraph to say all that you want to say, and rewrite your letter keeping in the essentials, throwing out words, sentences, and paragraphs that add little to the meaning.

The next day come back to your letter and continue paring it down until you know that, rather than saying everything, you have said enough to get the point across. Check your message for tone. If it's right, if you are satisfied with your letter, slip it through the mail slot.

Saturday night, late

Dear Clara,

I hate the computer. You know why? Because it's becoming my link to the loves in my life, when I wanted the link to be my arms. I thought that loving through cuddling could conquer everything and anything that might come along as a foe. I thought that my heart was enough. But I'm finding that it may not be. I didn't allow for the power in the other person's heart. I didn't allow for the punch that time brings to a situation. I believed in fairy stories and happy endings. I'd hoped for so much more.

Clara, I love you. I don't totally understand everything that this means. I just know it's true. I don't know why we were brought together, but I hold with faith that it was for a positive reason—for us both. I still see to the heart of you and see that you are loving and that there is something very special and very unique that we alone share. Do you want to fulfill the life goal of discovering with me why it was we came together? Even if you try, can you escape doing so? Are you trying? Trying to escape or to run toward me with open arms?

Tonight, Clara, I'm tired. I'm tired of working day and night at life. Tired of being in charge of myself and others. Tired of trying to be a responsible mom/employee/head of the household. And yet, when I look into your sister's eyes or think of your heart of hearts, I go on.

And before I lay down and crash into sleep, I wanted you to know that I've been thinking of you, kind of missing you, wishing that you'd finally "get it" and want to be loved back. That you'd finally trust someone enough, finally trust someone. That would be enough to start, and it's the starting that is so hard. And then the hour-by-hour trying that feels like an extraordinary, superhuman effort. And you get to wondering why. And if. And then what. And it's just so darned hard.

But Clara, I understand some of that. And I am here, doing the same.

Honest,

Mom

I love you.

Nudge 3

Choose another of your unsent letters, and rewrite it three times as if you were going to send it. With the first rewrite, think sensuous silk. Write the letter in a tone that feels soft to the touch, inviting, irresistible. With the second, write with a tone that feels like an overstarched linen shirt on your shoulders—stiff, unyielding, unnatural. With the third, write a letter that feels like a thick, rich wool sweater—heavy with warmth and presence.

If these comparisons do not work for you, write three letters that feel like (1) a hot fudge sundae, (2) a tamale with too many habaneros in the mix, (3) a plate of pickled pig's feet. The idea is to write your letter in three tones that would elicit totally different results. The goal of this nudge is, by exaggerating the tone of your practice letters, to become more aware of how your letter might either accomplish or sabotage your purpose for writing the letter.

After you have written three practice letters and read them aloud, use what you have learned about tone to write another draft of the letter you wish to send. Write and write until the letter contains a tone that suits your purpose. Note the insights you've gained concerning (1) the original tone you used for this letter, (2) the final tone you employed in writing it, and (3) how the two compare. If you are completely satisfied with your message, put on the stamp, and kiss the letter adieu.

Nudge 4

One of the most famous letters ever written was a question. In 1897, a little girl wrote:

"Dear Editor: I am 8 years old. Some of my little friends say there is no Santa Claus. Papa says 'If you see it in The Sun, it's so.' Please tell me the truth: is there a Santa Claus? Virginia O'Hanlon."

I don't know if little Virginia was afraid to ask her question, but I do know that sometimes we refrain from asking what our hearts want to know because we fear the answer. I guess each of us has to decide whether living without asking is better or worse than seeking the truth of the matter and, in the process, risking hurt or disappointment. Some of us like candles before they are burned, in their pure, clean, untested state. Some of us like them better after they've shed some light, now slightly melted, off balance, rife with proven character.

Experiment today with how it feels to pose a question. Recreate one of your unsent letters, but rather than stating your dilemma as a series of facts, describe the things you do not know about the problem and ask for help with filling in the blanks. It does not have to be a solution that you are seeking. More complete information could bring a feeling of resolution. So could having the recipient of your letter join you in the process of adding pieces to an incomplete puzzle.

As with other letters that you will send, take your time with this one. Write, wait for twenty-four hours, read your letter aloud, and rewrite until you know for certain that the message is ready to be mailed.

Final nudge: write a letter of homecoming

Today, as you work on a letter that has been writing itself in your mind for a long time, imagine yourself coming home. You open the door. The rooms are dark, silent, and cold. But with the flick of a switch, comfort returns. Familiarity. A well in the sofa's cushion waits for you like mashed potatoes awaiting gravy. A coffee cup on the counter reminds you of breakfast with family vying for favorite sections of *The Wall Street Journal.* An open book lying on the coffee table beckons you back to a blazing fire and to hours of adventurous escape that alight with the simple turning of a page. Pleasure in the form of tiny details joins together like patches of the worn but wonderful crazy quilt your grandmother made for you years ago.

It is in the details that we find meaning; in details that pattern us alongside people we love and things that hold comfort, memory, and promise. In letters that you cannot help but write, you gather up thoughts and feelings that have been wandering like souls lost in the thick of night. You give these disjointed memories and emotions order and, by sharing them with another person, a touch of immortality. You return to your center, return home to the things that mean the most to you as you pen your words and let them fly on their way to an anxiously awaiting heart.

So, pick up your pen, open the door to messages that refuse to remain silent, and write a letter. Connect the dots between who and what you are and who it is that helps to give your life meaning.

INDEX

Begin Your Self-Exploration Journey With Walking Stick Press

From Me to You—You long to express your feelings, share your memories, and thank those people who have helped you along the way. *From Me to You* provides the key to writing sincere personal messages, even if you struggle with getting words on paper. JacLynn Morris and Paul L. Fair mix friendly step-by-step instruction with model letters to help you to accurately express your sentiments of gratitude, sympathy, forgiveness, love, apology, and comfort.
ISBN 1-58297-004-1 ✳ paperback ✳ 192 pages ✳ #10706-K

Bliss—Bliss is fully engaging with your life to achieve emotional well-being, spiritual resonance, and psychological balance. You can attain bliss and experience greater personal fulfillment by learning who you really are and what you really want. Katherine Ramsland shows you how, mixing practical advice with dozens of illuminating writing activities. You'll discover the personal paths that will lead you to a happier, more productive life.
ISBN 0-89879-975-9 ✳ paperback ✳ 192 pages ✳ 10687-K

Memoirs of the Soul—You have a personal story to tell—one that illuminates who you are and how you arrived at this moment in your life. *Memoirs of the Soul* helps you to write about the times of wonder in your life: your strength, creativity, resilience, and moments of transformation. Doing so will breathe new life into personal memories, stimulate spiritual growth, and develop profound connections to the special places and people that have touched your heart.
ISBN 1-58297-080-7 ✳ paperback ✳ 224 pages ✳ 10764-K

Write Your Heart Out—Your best writing comes straight from the heart, filled with truth, imagination, and passion. *Write Your Heart Out* helps you better capture these qualities and use writing as an ongoing means of self-discovery and self-expression. Rebecca McClanahan does far more than just provide inspiration. She helps you examine the subjects you feel strongest about, then write about them with honesty and authority—for personal expression or publication.
ISBN 1-58297-006-8 ✳ paperback ✳ 224 pages ✳ 10735-K

Keeping a Journal You Love—Whether joyous, exciting, sad, or unexpected, the special moments of your life demand further exploration. In *Keeping a Journal You Love*, author Sheila Bender provides an encouraging mix of practical instruction, sample journal entries, and writing prompts that enables you to transform your journal into a personal, private sanctuary. In addition, fifteen other respected writers share their own journal entries along with enlightening commentaries.
ISBN 1-58297-068-8 ✳ paperback ✳ 240 pages ✳ 10750-K

A Year in the Life—*A Year in the Life* gently leads you through one full year of introspective writing, using weekly prompts and topics as a springboard into your deepest feelings. Sheila Bender provides the perfect blend of structure, guidance, and creative freedom, motivating you to begin writing today and continue on throughout the year with zest and satisfaction. And with the close of each season, she'll help you analyze what you've written to understand memories, feelings, and relationships as never before.
ISBN 0-89879-971-6 ✳ paperback ✳ 224 pages ✳ 10656-K

These books and other fine Walking Stick Press titles are available from your local bookstore, online supplier, or by calling 1-800-289-0963.